MAKING THE MOST OF STUDY ABROAD

MAKING THE MOST OF STUDY ABROAD

A Guide to a Top-Notch Experience

MELANIE L. D'AMICO AND

JOSHUA POPE

ROWMAN & LITTLEFIELD
Lanham • Boulder • New York • London

Published by Rowman & Littlefield
An imprint of The Rowman & Littlefield Publishing Group, Inc.
4501 Forbes Boulevard, Suite 200, Lanham, Maryland 20706
www.rowman.com
86-90 Paul Street, London EC2A 4NE

British Library Cataloguing in Publication Information Available

Library of Congress Cataloging-in-Publication Data
978-1-5381-8118-8 (cloth)
978-1-5381-8119-5 (electronic)

Contents

Chapter 1

Choosing the Right Program

Welcome to the exciting and enriching world of study abroad! We're glad you've decided to read our book and learn about how to get the very best experience from your international travels. Studying and traveling abroad is truly a transformative experience. It allows you to immerse yourself in a completely new way of life, allowing you to learn about another culture firsthand, see incredible sites, and meet people from around the globe. We hope that your time abroad will bring you some of your best moments and will provide you with an experience that stays with you throughout your life.

While our book is primarily directed to people who want to study in another country, we also include information that can apply to people who are traveling abroad for an extended period, including working abroad, volunteering abroad, and generally, living abroad. We know you must be excited (and maybe a little apprehensive) about your upcoming travels, just as we are excited to share with you our knowledge and expertise of the world of study abroad.

We, Melanie and Josh, are both university professors with many years of experience with international study and travel. As specialists in second language acquisition, we have researched the study abroad experience to achieve a better understanding of this unique learning context. Melanie has been fortunate to study abroad twice, once during her undergraduate work in Salamanca, Spain, and then again, during her graduate studies in Rome, Italy. She also leads a university summer program in Salamanca, Spain. Additionally, she has completed study abroad research in Costa Rica, France, Germany, Italy, and Spain. Her personal travels have also taken her to Belize, Canada, Greece, Honduras, Mexico, Portugal, Switzerland, Taiwan, and the United Kingdom. Melanie feels that studying and traveling abroad opens you up to new perspectives and provides you with a greater understanding of your place in the world. In many ways, her abroad experiences have helped shape her adult life and continue to bring new and interesting opportunities.

Josh was first introduced to the idea that someone could study in a different country when he received a flier about being a high school student in Australia. He wondered if that could happen and if it were feasible. Even though he still hasn't been to Australia (yet!), it should be no surprise that when he heard about a short-term study abroad program in Salamanca, Spain, at his undergraduate university, he jumped on it. A couple of years later, he spent a full academic year in Alcalá de Henares, Spain, as part of a graduate program. He has returned to Spain regularly since then to research, accompany students, and enjoy life. He has led groups of students to Mexico and Panama as well as enjoyed personal time in Ireland, Portugal, Greece, the Netherlands, Nicaragua, Belize, Honduras, Canada, and forty-eight of the fifty US states. At his current university, he advises students who wish to apply for postgraduate international fellowships and he temporarily worked as the co-director of study abroad. He can't imagine a life without travel and hopes to instill that drive in students and readers of this book.

Now that you know a little about us, here is what to expect in this book. Each chapter has a different theme, some with more of a practical side, and others with advice to help you with various aspects of international living. Depending on your personal needs, you might choose to read the book from cover to cover, or you might choose to skip around to the chapters that interest you the most. In this chapter, we tackle the first step, choosing the right program. We'll discuss how to research the myriad of programs available to you, what to consider for academics, thoughts about choosing a location, important information to consider for housing, and other key issues that arise with selecting the right host country for you.

Before we cover those topics, however, we want to spend a moment and talk about why you are choosing to go abroad. As part of planning your time abroad, you should take time to carefully consider what is compelling you to go. For some people, this may feel very straightforward at first because they are going abroad for a specific purpose, such as to learn a second language, to study at a particular school, or to work for a certain company. Nonetheless, beyond this big reason why you're going abroad, what are your other reasons for why you want to do this? How do you envision yourself while abroad? What are some important goals you have for your travels? We encourage you to reflect on your various motivations for going abroad to help you identify what you want to get out of your time in your host country. Some of the goals might be easier to name, activities like visiting famous sites or trying a particular sport could be of interest to you. Yet, some other aspects, like making friends in the host country, or finding a different lifestyle might be more nebulous and harder to define. It helps though to brainstorm about all of the various ideas you have about your travel abroad and to find a way to prioritize your goals. Taking the time to think about your reasons for going abroad will assist you in identifying specific facets of the type of programs available to you and help you eliminate ones that will not be as useful to meeting your goals. For example, suppose you want to experience a fast-paced, cosmopolitan lifestyle. You will want to look for programs that are in more urban areas that provide that type of experience. This would mean the difference in choosing a city like Milan over Florence. While both are in Italy and there will be cultural overlap between the two, there is a much different atmosphere in each of these two cities with Milan being the more modern, large city and Florence as the more historic, quaint one. Both places are culturally rich and provide memorable experiences, but one may be more suited to your vision of yourself abroad than the other.

WHERE DO I START?

Once you have decided that you are interested in studying abroad, it is logical that you will want to dive into finding a program. You may then find that there are either a large amount of programs in the place you want to study or perhaps even no programs. So where do you start to figure out what programs are available to you? The first thing you should do is visit your university's study abroad office. This office may be with other international programs, experiential learning programs, or go by a different name. Many universities' offices host study abroad fairs. This can be a good way to be introduced to them and to find sample programs. The reasons why it is important to start with this office involve their expertise. They know where to find appropriate programs for a wide range of students. They may even have preselected programs that offer the best academic and cultural experiences. Also, they will make your choices more manageable.

Your university's study abroad office will be a great resource since they will also know your home university's policies related to studying abroad. For example, universities will have a list of countries where they will not send students. Typically, they follow the US State Department travel advisories based on war, health and wellness, social unrest, and discrimination, among other reasons. Also, your university will surely have rules about the length of study abroad programs they will support, especially during the traditional academic year. Therefore, we highly recommend that you visit the study abroad office very early in your decision-making process.

Another good idea may be to ask one of your professors. Additionally, you should talk to a professor or advisor in your field since they will need to be a part of the discussion. After meeting with the study abroad office, it is good to speak with a knowledgeable professor and let them know about the programs you are considering. They will offer the insight they have and can help you narrow down your decision. Your academic advisor may also need to sign forms or approve your study abroad before you can finalize your plans.

PROGRAM TYPES

Study abroad programs can vary greatly in their appearance, structure, and offerings. In this section, we highlight a few common program types, particularly related to the amount and type of support you will get. First, in many cities that receive a large amount of students, there will be multiple program providers. At the time of this writing, some examples of such providers are WorldStrides and CIEE.[1] These program providers have local staff that will provide support to students related to their academics, housing, cultural and social events, and other administrative needs. In this type of program, there may be a group of American students with you. The structure these programs provide gives many students a sense of security, knowing that they have someone to whom they can ask questions. More independent students may feel like some of these programs are too involved in their lives, though. Another option you may want to ask your university's study abroad office about is a direct exchange program, such as ISEP.[2] These are typically agreements your home university has with an external partner to send and receive students.

A more independent student may want to consider a program without an in-country provider. You would enroll directly into a foreign university through that university's international

5

programs office. You need to be able to navigate the host university to register for classes, find housing, and meet people. This is not unattainable but could be difficult, especially if you are studying abroad in a country where you are not a very proficient speaker of the local language.

Finally, your home university may provide study abroad opportunities administered by someone in the university. These tend to be short-term summer programs like we have led with our students. Occasionally, universities may run longer-term programs. We know of one university's architecture school that sent a faculty member and students to Greece for a full semester. In this type of program, you would be more likely to know other people who go but you would also be avoiding any issues stemming from enrolling in a different school.

ACADEMIC CONSIDERATIONS

When researching your study abroad program, we advise you to carefully consider how many credits you want to take, and which courses will be the best options. First, thinking about the number of credits, we recommend you do not overload yourself with classes. Since you will want to be free to participate in activities in the community and to travel around your host country, you likely do not want this to be a semester where you take a high number of credits, if possible. Remember though that most universities will still require you to take the same minimum number of credits to be a full-time student, regardless of being abroad. This is particularly important if you are on a scholarship or other grant.

When selecting your courses for your study abroad, you should consider two main factors: what courses are unique to the study abroad location, and what courses will count toward your degree programs at your home university. Let's discuss uniqueness first. Often students feel they must follow a proposed degree plan to the letter, and they do not realize the flexibility that is available to them. Your study abroad semester is your chance to have more variation in your course offerings and to use your elective credits creatively. Study abroad offers you the opportunity to choose courses that are not typically taught (or not able to be taught) at your home institution. These are the courses that you should consider first as they will be more enriching to your overall degree. They may also give you a chance to study something new that you had never considered before. There is little point in taking a class abroad when its equivalent is offered at your home institution every year or every semester. Before you depart, we highly recommend that you take the time to speak to your advisor or the study abroad coordinator at your school about your courses. Don't be afraid to suggest taking the unique courses. Your advisor should be able to help you figure out how to count those unique courses in your program. Some universities even have special study abroad topics courses that can be used for your transcript.

Nonetheless, you do want to make sure you are taking courses that still relate to your programs of study. While you can use a wider definition of your chosen major or minor for your study abroad classes, you should still take classes that will help you toward earning your degree. This is particularly important when considering the level of the courses. Occasionally students try to take lower-level classes while abroad because they are concerned about maintaining their GPA or they see the semester abroad as being academically more relaxed. However, if you choose to do this, you can end up taking a bunch of classes that won't count for anything. Be sure to check with your advisor about the level of classes you need to be taking and stick to those when selecting your schedule. Additionally, make sure you are taking academic courses as opposed to extracurricular courses. Sometimes you will need to carefully read the course description and may need to request a syllabus for the course to guarantee it is acceptable for transfer credits. For example, if you choose to study abroad in Seville, Spain, you may have the opportunity to take courses about Flamenco dancing. Some of these courses are academically based, discussing the history and culture of Flamenco in Spain,[3] while others are extracurricular classes that teach you how to dance Flamenco. The history and culture class can count for transfer credit, but the dance class usually does not. Exceptions could be made if you are majoring or minoring in dance or performing arts.

For most universities, you will be required to provide a list of your intended courses before you go abroad. However, it is important to note that just as with your home institution, not all courses can be offered every semester. Therefore, it is prudent to select a few alternative courses if your first choices are not available. If course information such as a syllabus or course plan is provided, be sure to look it over carefully and do not pick your courses based on title alone. You might plan to sign up for a film course thinking that you will spend most of your time watching movies, only to find out that you also have to read several plays related to the films. Finally, when selecting courses, be sure to check the language of the course if you are studying in a country where English is not the primary language.

If you are planning to take courses in your second language, you will probably have to take a proficiency test to determine your appropriate level for courses. Occasionally this testing is done before your departure, but often it happens in the first few days of your arrival in your host country. You should be prepared to take both a written test and an oral interview as most programs will want to assess multiple skills before assigning you to a level. Do not be overly concerned about your level, especially if you feel you should be one level higher or lower than was determined for you. Nonetheless, if you find that in the first week of classes, your language level does not match that of the class, you could take the testing a second time and possibly be reassigned to a different level.

Before going abroad, you will need to review your school's policies and procedures for transferring credits. Most institutions are willing to work together for a successful transfer of credits, but depending on what relationship the two schools have, there may be more or less work for you to do. If your university has an exchange agreement in place with your host institution, then, likely, credit transfers have already been preapproved or a policy for transfer is already in place. Likewise, if you are working with a third-party exchange service or study abroad provider that is approved by your school, there should already be set rules for how to transfer your credits. In some cases, however, the responsibility is yours alone and you must keep careful records of your courses, the number of credits, your equivalent grades, similar courses at your home institution, and a detailed description of the courses. We recommend that everyone keep track of this information, as even in situations where a predetermined exchange agreement is in place, you may be asked to provide details of your courses for transfer to happen.

Also, before you go, be sure to ask about any courses that might be more difficult to transfer or that may not count in the way you hoped. For example, it is often not possible to take your general education courses abroad as those usually have specific course components that your university has predetermined. Additionally, there may be major-specific courses, often Capstone courses, that are required to be taken at your home campus. This is usually a concern if you are planning to go abroad in your final year, and should be considered as you make your plans to finish your studies.

As you research educational opportunities in your selected host country, you should note that there can be additional learning experiences available at different host institutions. These types of experiences include internships, experiential learning, volunteerism, and other varieties of alternative learning. For example, for students who are interested in a career in health or social services, there are often a variety of blended experiences that provide specialized courses along with hands-on experience in the community.[4] To facilitate the ability for foreign students to participate in these activities, most of these learning opportunities are designed as courses, and you may enroll in them as you would a typical class. Be aware though that some of these experiences require a separate application before you can join them.

LOCATION

When you are deciding where you would like to study abroad, it is pretty typical to consider countries. Someone interested in classic architecture may choose to study abroad in Greece while someone interested in learning Bengali may choose India. However, inside each country you will find a wide variety of lifestyles. Think about the United States. We all probably agree that life in Chicago and life in rural Peru, Illinois, are quite different although they are only one hundred miles apart. In addition to choosing a country, you should also research your options within that country. That way you know that Bengali is much more common in eastern India than in other parts of the country.

It is important to think about the pros and cons of choosing a rural or urban environment. Even more specific, do you want a medium-sized city or a large city? While large cities may provide more familiarity, more activities, and more people, we recommend that you pay serious attention to smaller cities. This doesn't necessarily mean tiny villages. Take for example Alicante, Spain. This has become a popular destination for Josh's students because of the reputation it has achieved on their home campus in Nebraska. The city has a population of around 330,000, enough that there are plenty of activities to do and connectivity to larger parts of Spain, all without what may be an overwhelming feeling of a large city like Barcelona. That city has a lot in common with Alicante but on a much larger scale.

You can also consider the types of transportation you are open to and comfortable using. First, think about how connected to the United States you want to be. If you choose to study abroad in Malaysia, just know that you may need to take several long flights to get there. Meanwhile, those studying in Mexico will take flights that are the same length as many domestic flights. Additionally, research the public transportation and pedestrian situations in your host city. Would you feel comfortable learning to take them? Notice we say "comfortable learning." By this we mean that you should learn to take public transportation as long as it's safe to do so. This is important because you will almost certainly be without a car during study abroad unless you are studying abroad in Canada.

Your choice of study abroad location may also be influenced by your tourism goals even though this shouldn't be your primary motivation. For example, if you plan to see major cities in a variety of countries, you may want to consider being based in a large city so that you have quick access to a large international airport.

HOUSING

There are typically three options for housing when studying or working abroad: homestays with a local family, student dormitories/apartments, and private apartments. Depending on your program and host country you may have the option to choose between all three but you also may only have one option available to you. This may factor into your decision for one program over another. As a student, generally you can only choose from those options that are preapproved by your program and your university. This is due to safety and legal issues related to student housing. In other words, you may not be able to choose your housing independent of your program. Let's consider each of these three housing styles and why you may or may not want to select them.

Homestays are with a local family that provides you with a room, meals, and basic cleaning; occasionally other services such as laundry are included. These are designed to give you direct contact with people from the host culture and to give you the experience of living with a real family. Homestay families can give you a chance to see and participate in regular cultural practices of everyday life in your host country. If you are in a non-English speaking country, the host families will speak to you in the local language and encourage you to practice the language with them. Host families must be fully vetted by the host institution or international student program to be approved to house international students. Most host families host two international students at a time, usually from the same program or home country. Some host families strive to make you feel like a member of the family, having meals with you, spending time with you, and sometimes inviting you to participate in a family event. Other host families are more hands-off, and while you will spend time with them in the house or during meals, you may not develop a close relationship. You should note that host families will have house rules (such as removing your shoes in the house or not using the kitchen after a certain hour) and you will need to follow them. There are usually designated quiet hours and you will need to be responsible for checking in with your host family if you are not coming home for a meal or will be going away for a weekend. If you are particularly interested in improving your language skills and learning about culture, we recommend a homestay as your first choice of housing. If you are working abroad for a shorter period, homestays may also be available to you. You can check with your employer or international workers' groups about this housing option.

At some host institutions, student dormitories or apartments may be available. Similar to here in the United States, these are owned by the institution and are strictly for students attending the school. This housing can be for all students, domestic and international, or is sometimes only for international students. Many of these types of stays include some type of cooking facility as you will be responsible for all of your own food shopping and meal preparations. (Although not common, some student housing comes with a cafeteria for meals.) You are also usually responsible for doing your own basic cleaning of your room or apartment. Roommates are typically assigned at random through the university (again similar to the United States). With this type of student housing, you will have more independence but you will need to follow the host institution's rules for the dormitory or apartment (such as no candles or no overnight guests). Staying in student housing is a good way to meet other students, especially local students if the housing is open to them. There are typically shared spaces that allow for hanging out and spending time together. One major difference to consider between US student housing and study abroad student housing is that the study abroad institution may not be in the same location as the housing. In other words, living in student housing does not mean you will be living on campus. International universities do not tend to have campuses like those here in the United States where everything is contained in the same main area. Instead, your student housing may be across town from where you take your classes. If you are working abroad, your employer may have some type of employee housing that is similar to student housing at a university and you may want to ask about that option.

Private apartments are another common option for studying abroad and are often the only option for working abroad. For students, these can be arranged through the host program, but they may require additional work on your part for the initial setup. For example, you may be asked to pay a security deposit separate from your host institution fees. (In the case of a third-party provider, this should be handled for you and you only make payments to the provider.) As with finding an apartment at home, you will likely have roommates, either international like you or local people. Different from student apartments, your roommates can be anyone living in the community and they may be quite different in age from you. For example, when studying in Rome, Melanie's classmate (age twenty-two at the time) shared an apartment with two women, one in her thirties and the other in her forties. This type of living situation affords you the most independence. You will be responsible for your meals and cleaning and will (likely) decide on any apartment rules with your roommates.

In her research into study abroad, Melanie has discovered that many students choose private apartments or student housing over homestays because they value independence more than anything. However, in speaking to students at the end of their programs, most talked about how nice it would have been to be able to connect more with locals. Students who lived with local students or in homestays shared that they felt they had made deeper connections with the local community through their housing situation. Additionally, students from student housing and apartments expressed the idea that having meals and cleaning provided was very attractive to them. Several students mentioned the difficulty in navigating food markets and smaller grocery stores to get what they needed, especially when doing so with only public transportation. On the other hand, students from homestays often commented on how much they enjoyed having a break from having to cook and clean for themselves, and how much they were able to learn about local cuisine from their host families.

OTHER CONSIDERATIONS

In addition to the topics we have already discussed, there will surely be others that will affect your choice of study abroad program. It is not possible to list each factor because you need to pick one that works best for you. In this section, we attempt to round out what we see as common factors to consider when making your choice.

First, there will be cultural factors to consider. By this, we mean a wide variety of things. You may already realize that one of your biggest goals during study abroad is to learn from people of diverse cultures and to live among such cultural differences that they provoke a type of culture shock, which will be detailed in chapter 4. However, you do still need to research your potential host countries to make sure you would be a good fit for that culture. Doing so isn't just for comfort's sake. Choosing a good cultural fit may also affect your safety. For example, if you hold certain religious beliefs as essential to your identity and you can't imagine not outwardly demonstrating them, it would not be a good idea, nor potentially a safe idea, for you to study abroad in a community where that religion may be looked down upon. Instead, look around for a place where you would be welcomed for who you are. This may even be in the same country! Another example can relate to how prepared you feel to be independent. If you have never been abroad before, you may not feel very comfortable studying abroad in a rural setting in a country where the cultural differences are vast compared to your home. You may prefer a program that has a bit more in common with what you are accustomed to. Again, this may even be in the same country! Be mindful of culture but accept and appreciate that you will be uncomfortable with some of the cultural differences you encounter.

The final factor that we will focus on here is cost. Studying abroad is expensive so your choice will likely involve a discussion of finances with your university and your family. When it comes to costs, there are a few good things to consider. First, studying abroad does not have to be a full academic year or even a semester. Short-term study abroad during a summer term is a better option for some. You may even find a good month-long program that fulfills your goals and curricular needs. Shorter stays may mean lower costs. Additionally, you may be able to apply financial aid to your study abroad program, especially if it is a requirement for your academic program. We know of universities that allow students who are required to study abroad for academics to take 100 percent of their institutional financial aid for the costs of their program. Every school is different, though. You may be able to also use your student loans to defer the cost of studying abroad. There are other funding options as well, including scholarships from program providers and even the US government. For example, students who are eligible for the Pell Grant based on family income are also eligible to apply for the Gilman Scholarship and students whose parents are in the military may apply for the Gilman-McCain Scholarship, both of which help alleviate the financial costs of study abroad and work to make such experiences more accessible.[5] Therefore, bring in your financial aid office to help you understand what your situation is.

In this chapter, we hope to have given you some direction to make a programmatic choice. In the rest of the book, we explore other parts of the study abroad experience, from the pre-departure preparation to the experience itself, even to the post–study abroad return. The book is designed to be read in the order that you need to read it. It makes sense to read it from front to back but it also makes sense to jump around. Now, let's go abroad.

CHAPTER 2

Administrative and Logistical Issues

ONCE YOU'VE MADE THE EXCITING DECISION TO STUDY ABROAD
and have chosen a destination, the last thing you probably want
to do is a lot of tedious paperwork, reading, and other legal stuff.
If this describes you, unfortunately, you still have to do it. This
chapter is meant to give you some things to think about as you
prepare for the legal aspects of study abroad. Some of the content
isn't as exciting as in other chapters and some of it is downright
unpleasant but we bring these topics up because they are crucial.
In this chapter, you'll read about several things you should do
before, during, and after study abroad. You will surely need to do
more than the tasks included here, depending on your citizenship,
your destination, your university, or other factors.

PREDEPARTURE
Passports and Visas
A passport is a document, usually in book format, that proves
your citizenship. Before we begin telling you about the passport
process, we want to point out that we are writing about these processes as they pertain to US citizens. If you are not a US citizen,
you will need to seek out additional materials. Unless you already
have a passport, you need to start the process of getting one as
soon as you decide that you are going to study abroad, perhaps

even as soon as you start considering study abroad as an option. Typically, the US State Department gives a time frame of eight to twelve weeks to process a passport application but this may vary. This doesn't include mailing times. However, you must also take into consideration that you will need that passport before you start your visa paperwork. If you already have a passport, you need to make sure that it is valid for a long enough time. For many countries, you will be denied entry if your passport expires even a few months after your visa period ends. Josh once spoke to a woman who was not able to enter a country that required six months of passport validity because her passport would expire two days shy of that requirement. Therefore, this is something that you need to be responsible and proactive about.

The process for US citizens applying for a passport is outlined on the State Department's website.[1] In this paragraph, we summarize the process in place at the time of this writing. If you are applying for your first passport, you will need to complete and turn in the appropriate form found on travel.state.gov, a photo, and a fee of $130. The photo must be recent, be two inches by two inches, show your whole face clearly and without a filter, and it needs to be against a white background. You are not allowed to take a selfie or wear glasses for your passport photo. Some clothing, such as camouflage, is also prohibited. One of the easiest ways to get an appropriate passport photo is to go to a store that provides photo services. In many cases, they will already have an acceptable background, camera, and printer so that you get a good photo within minutes. You will take these materials to an acceptance facility near you (an appointment is usually required). The State Department's website has a search function to help you find such a facility but many are located in post offices, libraries, or other local government buildings. In addition to turning in your form, photo, and fee, you will also need to show proof that you are a US citizen (e.g., birth certificate or certificate of naturalization) and show a second photo ID (e.g., state-issued ID). The process to renew your passport is similar except that you may not need the in-person appointment and may be able to apply via mail. As of the time of this writing, the State Department is piloting an online renewal program but is not currently available on a widespread basis. Do note that this is a summary of the passport application process. You should check out travel.state.gov to read about specifics and to see if you have any special considerations.

The next step is to ensure that you will be studying in your host country legally. You should check with your host program for their guidance about what type of visa you will need. It is possible that you do not need a visa beyond a tourist visa, especially if you are doing a short program. However, for programs that are at least a semester, you will likely need a student visa. It is impossible for us to list everything that you'll need to do when applying for a visa to every country. Instead, we provide you here with some general information and one country's example. In many countries, a student visa allows you to complete an academic program or coursework in the host country. In most cases, you are allowed to travel around and outside of the host country during the course of your stay. You may find that your student visa has restrictions on employment. You may be allowed to work a limited number of hours, have that employment be restricted to something related to your academics, or be completely prohibited. When you apply for your visa, you will need to provide information about yourself, your citizenship, your academic program, your health insurance, and your finances, among other things. You may need to provide proof that you are healthy and do not have a criminal record. Travel to an embassy or a consulate may even be required. For example, many students in the Midwest who study in Spain will need to travel to the Spanish Consulate in Chicago at least once. Some countries may approve you for a temporary student visa. If this is the case, you may need to complete additional steps once you are in the country.

Let's take a closer look at the application process for a student visa to Australia, a common host country for American students. This is meant to be an overview. You need to take a closer look at the requirements if you are applying for a visa to Australia. Australia's Department of Home Affairs provides detailed information about the process and documentation required on its website.[2] You can complete this application completely online from outside of Australia. You need to provide a great deal of information such as what is listed in the previous paragraph. You may need to have a health exam and will also need to acknowledge that you read their booklet about Australian values and principles. Once you have submitted your application, Home Affairs may ask for additional information, such as specifics of your criminal record. As of spring 2023, Australia charges 650 Australian dollars ($437 USD) to apply for the visa. Once your visa is approved, it is completely electronic. Border officials will be able to see your approved student visa when you enter the country.

If you are abroad for a primary reason other than to study, your visa process will look different. This will be the case for sojourns related to work, research grants, and volunteerism, among others. Like with a student visa, you will need your sponsor organization to play a major part in your visa process. You should be proactive about the type of visa needed and should keep in frequent communication with the people who will help you through the process.

Preparing to Enter Your Host Country
If you have never been to a different country, you may be feeling anxious about what passport control and customs are like. First, know that related terminology can vary widely around the world. It is a good idea to research your host country's entry-related terms so that you know what to do when you arrive. For example, some countries use terms like immigration or migration while others use passport control and/or customs. The meaning of

customs may include passport control or it may only refer to the area where you declare what you are bringing into the country (see more later). Since there will be a wide variety of procedures, please take what we write in these sections as general guidance and not as a strict description of what will happen.

When you fly to a different country, you will quickly notice one additional step that you don't have to do when you fly domestically. You will need to show your passport to the airline when you check in (and maybe even when you board the plane). They have to make sure that you have the correct documentation to enter your country before you get there. Once you arrive in your host country, you will not disembark into a large, busy gate area. You will typically be led into a separate pathway that leads to passport control or customs. This is where you will show your passport and/or visa. You may be asked to provide information about your lodging (have the address ready), length of stay, return flight, and purpose of travel, among other information. Some countries want you to provide this information on paper, some verbally, and some may have an app. Be flexible and listen closely to any instructions given to make sure you go through smoothly. Some countries may charge a fee at this stage as well. Research before your arrival will tell you if this is expected. After you pass through this stage, you will probably collect your checked luggage, even if you have a connecting flight, before you pass through an area where you are asked if you have any money or items to declare (listed by the country). Typically, you will not have anything to declare unless you have brought food or agricultural items with you. If you are at your final destination, you're done at this point. If you are continuing to another city, you'll drop off your luggage again and go on to your next gate. As you can guess, this process takes time. It's not abnormal to wait an hour or more, plus you may have to walk considerable distances. Therefore, if you have a connecting flight, it is important to ensure that you have a layover that is long enough to make it through immigration.

Arriving in much of Europe has an added complexity. If you are studying abroad, for example, in Copenhagen, Denmark, you may very well have a connecting flight through a larger city like Amsterdam, Paris, or Frankfurt. If this is the case, you will go through passport control and customs in the first European city and not in Copenhagen. This is because many European countries, including Denmark, the Netherlands, France, and Germany, are all within the Schengen Area, a group of countries that have open borders. This means that flying from Germany to Denmark is much like flying from Nebraska to Indiana. This is important to remember because you need to allow yourself time to go through customs in Paris before you go on your flight to Copenhagen.

Currency

At some point, you will want to get cash in the local currency. You should not assume that your US dollars will be useful in your host country unless you are going to a place that uses the dollar extensively, like Panama. In most international airports, there are booths where you can exchange your dollars for the local currency. Other options to do this will be to use an ATM or go to a place that does currency exchange outside of the airport. You may get differing exchange rates in the different options. You should research where the best place to exchange cash is in your host city. If you are planning to use an ATM most of the time, make sure you inform your bank. Also, plan to exchange some of your money at the airport so that you have enough cash to get where you are going. You may also wish to exchange money prior to your departure at your home bank. This can be done by most banks but will generally require an appointment and waiting period for the bank to obtain the foreign currency. Be aware too that banks may have a minimum amount required to exchange. As a tip, if you are traveling to a major city for a consulate or embassy visit to obtain your visa, you might want to also schedule a trip to a major bank for your currency exchange since most currency is more readily available in large city banks.

In addition to using cash, you may be able to use credit and debit cards in your host country. You must not assume this will be the case, though. Research how widely credit cards are used and in what types of transactions they are used in that country. For example, in Mexico, you can expect to use a credit card in a hotel or a larger restaurant in a city. However, you will need cash for the majority of your transactions, such as buying tickets to an archeological site. Even when we were studying abroad in Spain in the early 2000s, we always needed to assume we would use cash except for large transactions. You'll even notice differences in how businesses take cards. In restaurants, many servers will bring a card reader to your table because, to many non-Americans, it is unheard of that a server would take your credit card away from you to process your transaction. As mentioned earlier, make sure to let your credit and debit card banks know what your travel itinerary is. This way, they can expect you to be there and they won't automatically decline your transactions.

Information from the US State Department

The US State Department provides information about the safety of traveling to other countries and regions within those countries. On their website,[3] they have four levels of advisory, coded both by color and number. Level one is blue and advises travelers to "exercise normal precautions"; level two is yellow and indicates "exercise increased caution"; level three is orange and advises travelers to "reconsider travel"; and level four is red and says "do not travel." The criteria the State Department uses to determine the advisory level depends on numerous factors, such as violence, conflict, and health. During the height of the COVID-19 pandemic, most of the world was labeled as level four advisory. For some countries, the State Department breaks their advisories up into regions. For example, they identify the label of each state in Mexico because there is a wide variety of risks throughout that large country. You should always know the advisory level of your host region. However, it is important to note that most study abroad providers will not run programs in places that have a level four advisory, or potentially a level three advisory.

The United States has embassies in capitals around the world and consulates in many other large cities. Embassies and consulates provide services to US citizens who are traveling abroad. Those services may include assistance if you have an issue with local authorities, help during natural disasters or social or political unrest, and help if you have lost your passport, among other things. Before you leave, familiarize yourself with the closest embassy or consulate by checking out their website, contact information, and location. It may be a good idea to copy that information down and keep it in your wallet so that you can easily refer to it in an emergency.

The US State Department also offers a free program called the Smart Traveler Enrollment Program (STEP) that allows you to register with the local US embassy or consulate of your destination country.[4] To use STEP, you will create an account either on the STEP website (step.state.gov/step/) or download the State Department's Smart Traveler app. Once you have your account, you will be able to add your trip details so that the local embassy or consulate can contact you in case of an emergency. STEP will also send you updates on other important information during your study, for example, when the embassy may be closing for a holiday. Don't worry if you don't have all your information right away, such as a local phone number. You will be able to edit and add information as you receive it. There is also a place for you to provide the information for your safety contacts. This is a helpful step in case someone from the embassy or consulate needs to contact them and you are not able to provide the information yourself.

Healthcare

To enter many countries, you may be required or highly advised to prepare medically. Usually, this is in the form of vaccines. You should discuss with your doctor and your program provider and consult with the US Centers for Disease Control (CDC) website to decide which vaccines you should get and what additional health measures you should take before, during, and after your stay abroad.[5] The CDC's Traveler's Health website is easy to use and provides a comprehensive look into what you need to do before going abroad. When you go to the site, you can enter the country you are going to. Let's use Panama as an example. When we select that country in their drop-down menu, we see a list of diseases that visitors should be vaccinated against. Beyond routine vaccinations that most Americans already have, the CDC recommends several additional vaccines, including Hepatitis A, Hepatitis B, and Typhoid, among others. They also recommend antimalaria treatment for certain regions.

You can get these travel vaccines at numerous places. Your primary care physician can be a good resource to help you decide which treatments to receive, especially if the CDC is just giving you guidance rather than a requirement. They can also be your source for getting your shots. Other options include local health departments, retail pharmacies, and clinics. For example, the University of Nebraska runs a clinic that is dedicated primarily to giving travel vaccines. They can access all the information you need about your destination, the risks associated, and the precautions needed. Check out large universities in your area, even if you aren't a student there, to see if there is a similar resource close by. One more thing: your normal health insurance may very well cover all or part of the costs of your vaccines.

Before your departure, you should also make sure that you are aware of what insurance needs you should consider. First, find out what your US health insurance will cover for you while you are abroad. Also, find out what your insurance provider needs you to do if you file a claim while you're abroad. You may need to buy a supplemental policy to cover any travel needs, whether they be health-related or not. It will be important to not only consider what type of medical treatment you are covered for while abroad but there are additional considerations too. It's not fun to think about but you need to be aware of what happens if you are in a coma or die while abroad. It costs a lot of money to transport a body. Therefore, you need to make sure you have a policy that covers the repatriation of your remains in the event that you die.

Many countries' healthcare systems work very differently from what you may be used to in the United States. It is important to know how health systems work so that you can minimize surprises. We know of someone who took a trip to Bali while studying abroad in Australia. In Bali, she was bit by a monkey but she waited until after she had returned to Australia to go to the doctor. Let's just say she ended up with some surprises that she would've liked to have been prepared for. These differences may be related to who pays for healthcare, how they pay for healthcare, who provides that care, and where you go to get it. Universal healthcare is a phrase you may have heard before. It relates to a system in which people can get the care they need without having to pay out of pocket. In some countries with universal healthcare, it may be citizens or permanent residents who benefit while visitors and temporary residents, like students, do not. In other places, students studying abroad may have access to the local healthcare system. You should research your host country's system with your study abroad office, host country administration, and any other important parties.

If you do need medical care, you will need to know where and how to get that care. Do you go to a doctor's office, a pharmacy, or a hospital? Do you need an appointment? In some countries, your first stop will be a pharmacy. In such places, there may be pharmacies in many parts of your host city. If they aren't able to help you, they can give you an idea of where you should seek additional care. In some places, you'll need to see a doctor but you may go to an actual hospital, rather than a clinic, to see that doctor. This is where your host institution's international student office or your study abroad provider may come in very handy. They are likely used to helping students navigate the local healthcare system. Some of them may be willing to accompany students to the doctor's visit. If you are working abroad, you might ask your employer for assistance, particularly your human resources contact. If you are unable to find someone to talk to at your university or job, try to find some information in a guidebook or a reputable website or walk into any kind of healthcare facility and ask what you should do.

Choosing Your Courses
Since your study abroad experience will involve taking courses, you will need to work with your study abroad office, your academic advisor, and your study abroad provider to pick courses that are right for you. Doing this before study abroad will allow you time to make sure the courses you choose will transfer correctly to your home university, will count for what you need, and are generally appropriate. You will likely need to maintain some flexibility in course selections since you may not know for sure what classes you will take until you arrive.

WHILE ABROAD
Learning and Abiding by New Laws
While you are abroad, you are not under the jurisdiction and protections of US laws. Instead, you will be responsible for following the laws of the host country. This means you need to be aware of laws that are relevant to you and your activities. Typically, when students who are studying abroad have problems with the law, it is usually related to drugs and alcohol. Many American students will assume that several host countries have more permissible laws regarding substances. They may believe that age restrictions

are not enforced or that marijuana is legal in all areas. This is not necessarily the case. To avoid problems with the law, find out what substances are legal in your host country, who can consume them, and in what contexts they can be consumed. For example, it may be legal in some countries for eighteen-year-olds to drink beer in their home with their families but not legal for them to drink with their friends in a park. Once you know the laws regarding drugs and alcohol, do not ignore them. Be very careful to follow them. If you are arrested while abroad, you will go through the host country's judicial system. The US embassy can provide support, such as helping find a lawyer, but you are ultimately responsible for your defense.

You may be surprised by what some countries consider a crime. Even in 2023, many countries continue to criminalize either identifying as LGBTQ+ or acting upon those identities. This means that an act like hand-holding could potentially lead to legal problems. If you identify as LGBTQ+, you should consider the legality of your identity when you are deciding where to study abroad. If you decide to still go to such a country, you need to remember to act in a way that will keep you safe and secure. The International Lesbian, Gay, Bisexual, Trans, and Intersex Association (ILGA) website provides information and a database that can help you gain the facts you need.[6]

In addition to considering laws that are new to you, you also need to keep in mind that social norms in certain countries may be different than what you are accustomed to. This can be related to public drug and alcohol use. For now, let's stick with the example of LGBTQ+ identities. You should know how your host country usually perceives people who identify as LGBTQ+, even if there are no crimes associated with it. If you choose to go to a country where homophobia or transphobia are societal norms in some pockets of the host country, you need to plan for how you can protect yourself. Even if you feel you can authentically express yourself in your home community in the United States despite potential negative societal consequences, it may not be a good idea to do so in your host country. It may be worth considering a different country if being yourself could lead to you getting hurt or having trouble with the law. Consult your study abroad office, your host institution, or an LGBTQ+ source in the country for help deciding.

If you are approached by the police while abroad, the most important thing to remember is to stay calm and follow their instructions. If you do not understand them, do your best to indicate this to the police. A woman we know was traveling in Italy and was approached by the police because they wanted to inform her that there was a gas leak in the area. She became very nervous because they were speaking in Italian, and she decided her best course of action was to run from them! This was a very poor decision as it ended up with the police chasing after her and almost detaining her due to her very strong reaction to them. Fortunately for her, one of the officers spoke enough English to understand that she was simply scared and she did not get into worse trouble. In the unfortunate event that you are arrested, again, do your best to remain calm and ask to contact the US embassy. We also recommend that you exercise your right to silence if that is granted to you. Many countries have similar Miranda rights to the United States.[7] If you are detained by the police, it is better to wait for your embassy representative or legal counsel to arrive before providing information.

Residency

When your host country approved your student, or tourist, visa, it did so only for a certain period. If you are traveling under a student visa, your time frame may mirror the amount of time you anticipate needing to complete your program. It may also only cover you for a certain period of months, regardless of how long you plan to stay. It is not legal for you to overstay your visa's legal time frame. Doing so could lead to you getting prosecuted and deported. You can avoid these legal residency issues by being aware of how long your visa is valid for and being proactive about any renewals. If you are abroad under a student visa, your host program, and perhaps your home university, will likely be involved with your visa renewal.

Working
In addition to being aware of how long you are allowed to stay in your host country, you should also be aware of what kind of work you can do while abroad. It may be tempting to find a job since it costs a lot of money to study abroad and you may be interested in doing some expensive travel. In most situations, you will not be able to take just any typical job because you will not have a work visa. However, you may be allowed to take a type of job meant for students such as a research or teaching assistantship or a job with a university office. Before you consider doing this, you should meet with your study abroad office at home and your host international programs office and refer to national laws about your visa to determine if you are allowed to work in that capacity. It may be possible to be employed by a US employer while you are abroad. For example, Josh was employed by his home university in the United States while he was studying abroad in Spain. His job was to tutor other American students who were in the Spanish program. He was paid in dollars and the checks were deposited directly into his American bank account. Again, you must verify that this is legal before you accept any kind of arrangement.

Connection to the United States
As mentioned previously, a US embassy (in a capital city) or consulate (in other cities) is an important connection to the United States while you're abroad. Their property is protected and cannot be entered by the host country without permission. They can help you if you lose your passport, need help finding legal representation and advocacy, and help you evacuate, among other services.

Familiarize yourself with the closest embassy or consulate and store their address and phone number in a safe place.

POST–STUDY ABROAD
Reentry to the United States
So, it's time to come back to the United States. If you have never traveled abroad before, you may wonder what the process of reentering the United States is like. If you are a US citizen, you just need your passport. If you are not a US citizen, you need the documentation that allows you to enter. Please research your particular case to make sure you know what you need to enter the United States.

There are a few different processes that you may encounter when going through passport control and customs while entering the United States. In most cases, you will go through these processes at the first American airport you get to. For example, if you are flying home to Oklahoma City after studying abroad in Tokyo, you may first land in a city like San Francisco. In such cases, you will go through passport control and customs in San Francisco before you go on your flight to Oklahoma. Note that this may take a lot of time. When you are booking your flight home, make sure you have a few hours to do everything you need to do in your first American airport. In some limited cases, such as returning from some Canadian and Irish airports, you will go through US passport control and customs before you even leave that country. This means you will not need to do so in the United States. You'll get off your plane at a normal gate like domestic flights. Wherever it is that you go through this process, here is essentially what happens. Note that this is meant to be general and there may be some variation depending on where you land, who your agent is, or other particulars. When your international flight arrives in the United States, you will deplane into a secure area meant to connect such flights with passport control. You will not have access to the rest of the airport until after you clear customs. The first place you'll come to is passport control. Here, you have a choice in many airports. You can do it the traditional way by waiting in line to see a human agent. You may also use the US Customs and Border Control Mobile Passport Control app. To do this, download the app and enter your information before going through passport control. This will include scanning your passport with your phone's camera. Once this is done correctly, you'll get a QR code which you can show to an agent. After this, you'll probably collect any checked luggage, go through customs where you declare what you have brought back (usually nothing major to declare), and you'll recheck your luggage. Once this is done, you'll be clear of customs. However, this area will feed you into an unsecured part of the airport. If you are continuing onto another US city, you will need to go through airport security again before you get to your next gate. As we said earlier, make sure you have time to do all of this.

Once you're back in the United States, you will also need to exchange any foreign currency back into US dollars. Like in other countries, you can do so at many large airports and in some banks. With that said, what you may want to do is try to plan your cash spending so that you are using the last of it as you arrive at the airport, ready to leave your host country. We have had many extra meals and coffees at airports just to get rid of the last of our cash. If you are unable to do this, you could also save the cash if you anticipate returning to your host country or you could sell it to someone else who is about to go somewhere where they could use that currency.

Academic Credit Transfer

One of the final things you will need to do after studying abroad is to make sure your academic credits have transferred to your home university. In many cases, especially when you've studied abroad with a provider or an office that frequently works with international students, you may not have to do much. In other cases, you will need to be more proactive about having your transcript sent to the United States. We do warn you, though, that transcripts can take a long time to be sent. We have both had students who studied abroad in the first semester of their senior year who were stressed out when their international transcripts cut it close to the time they needed them to graduate.

We hope this chapter has demystified many of the hard parts of preparing and going through the logistics of study abroad. We know we cannot cover it all. Combining the guidelines we've presented, along with any instructions you get from your study abroad office or host country administration, we hope you can enter, stay, and leave your host country smoothly.

CHAPTER 3

Packing

WHAT TO BRING AND WHAT TO LEAVE HOME

This chapter is a practical one that will give you advice for packing and the attention you should give to the personal belongings you choose to bring with you on your travels. Whether you are a seasoned traveler or new to travel, there are many aspects to consider when packing for a longer stay in a foreign country.

PACKING FOR LONG-TERM TRAVEL

As soon as you hear the phrase "long-term travel," you are likely to think that you need to plan to bring quite a variety of clothing, shoes, and other personal items for your sojourn away. However, the first rule of packing for this type of travel experience is that you need less than you think. We recommend that you lay out everything you think you need, then immediately take away half of it. This sounds drastic at first, but unless you are already an exceptionally light packer, there is a strong tendency for people to take too much with them when they travel internationally for long periods. (You can also start with our packing list at the end of the chapter.) Remember that you will have access to laundry facilities and you will likely purchase new things while you are abroad. Even if you think, "I'll simply ship home things I don't need," rethink this since international shipping can be very expensive and sometimes slow and is generally not recommended. Also please remember that your living accommodations may be smaller than you are used to with limited storage space.

Most international flights will allow you to have one personal item (backpack, tote bag, purse), one carry-on bag, and one checked bag free of charge (although watch out for new budget international travel that might not include luggage in your flight price). We recommend including one outfit and a couple of pairs of underwear in your carry-on luggage in case there is a delay with your checked baggage. Also, be sure to pack any essential items, like medication and some toiletries, in your carry-on bag or personal item. Many international flights are long and may last overnight. You might want to consider bringing a small travel pillow, earplugs, and a sleep mask to help you sleep better on the flight.

When packing for your travel, you might want to consider using packing cubes or packing bags that can help keep your items organized. These can be very helpful too in keeping things organized in your living space. Some packing cubes or bags also offer compression and can help you fit more into your luggage. Nonetheless, be sure to still consider the overall weight of your items as there are limits to the weight of your luggage for commercial flights and sometimes packing cubes cause you to bring too much!

When selecting your suitcases or backpack, make sure that you can move all your luggage by yourself for at least a couple of city blocks. We recommend taking your packed luggage on a walk through your neighborhood before you leave. You should also try to go up and down a flight of stairs with your luggage. It might sound silly to practice like this, but you will probably find there are a few more items you can remove, or you might realize you need a different style of bag. Many international cities have infrastructure that differs from the United States and there might not be easily accessible elevators or escalators. (If you have mobility or accessibility needs, you should carefully research your destination for the options that will be available to you.) You should also consider that you might be responsible for getting yourself to your local residence once you arrive. If you need to take public transportation to that residence, such as a metro, you will need to maneuver your luggage through the station, and on and off the train by yourself. Be wary of anyone offering you help with your luggage at the airport or around public transportation, they may expect you to pay them for their help, or in the worst case, they may simply run off with your luggage!

A general rule to keep in mind as you are selecting the items you wish to bring with you is durability and usability. You will want items that can stand up to travel and packing, and luggage that will be placed in a variety of spots throughout your travel (overhead bins or racks, bus or train luggage compartments, in the trunk of a car, or even on your lap). When it comes to clothing, you should consider that laundry facilities will be different while abroad. This is not the time to bring your most delicate clothing or pieces that need special care. Dry cleaning is available in many international locations but is not always common in some areas, so if you do need to bring dry-clean-only items, you should research the availability before your departure. For other items, consider the use you will get out of them and how frequently you intend to use them. Say, for example, you have a pair of shoes you only wear with one or two outfits. It would not be practical to bring those with you, as you are not likely to wear them regularly. Or perhaps you have a Bluetooth keyboard for your laptop that you sometimes use. It would probably be best to leave that at home, as your laptop's keyboard will be sufficient for your time abroad. This will save you from considering how to protect the keyboard from travel and will save you the luggage space for such a bulky item.

CHOOSING THE RIGHT CLOTHING

Fashion and clothing styles can and do vary greatly across the world, and it is beneficial to research your destination as you consider what clothing you want to pack. This does not mean that you need to go out and buy all new clothes or worry about dressing exactly like a local. However, this does mean being more aware of how you can stand out as a foreigner. For example, in many areas wearing t-shirts with English, athletic shoes, and baseball caps is an automatic sign that you are an American abroad. Similarly, wearing athletic clothing outside of a gym or sports venue is another common sign that you are an American. A good way to see how locals dress is to look online at mid-priced stores in the area and see what items are for sale. For example, if you are traveling to Europe you might consider looking at the department store Zara, which can be found in many countries, to see popular styles. You can also follow social media accounts for your destination and look through those to see how locals appear to be dressed (although be aware that if you are looking at tourist spots you might not be seeing locals).

Additionally, you should consider that there could be differences in modesty for your destination. This rule may be more applicable to women, however, men should also consider that some items that seem innocuous in the United States such as running shorts or muscle tanks, might be thought of as inappropriate in other countries. For women, dressing more modestly may also be a safety issue and serve as a way to minimize drawing unwanted attention to yourself. While you may feel perfectly comfortable in your shortest shorts at home, in another country those shorts might be a novelty and people may comment on them (sometimes in a very rude way). Again, even clothing that feels normal at home might not be common in the country you are visiting so doing your research before you go is ideal. In warmer weather, you may find that local people wear lighter clothing but not necessarily shorts or shorter skirts. If people do wear shorts, there is a tendency for them to be more tailored or in a slightly dressier material. Likewise, sleeveless garments may or may not be common. Also consider if you will be visiting any religious sites (temples, churches, shrines, cathedrals, etc.) as there are often special rules about how to dress when visiting. Frequently this means being more modestly dressed such as covering your arms or head with a shawl, not wearing hats inside, and sometimes removing your shoes before entering. Most attractions and local tourism offices can provide you with information, either online or in print, about visiting these places and making sure you have the proper attire. As with visiting religious sites, you will find that modesty rules may vary greatly depending on your location and activity. Wearing skimpy swimsuits or even going topless may be common on many European beaches, but as soon as people are off the beach you will see that they cover up when going back into town.

A good rule of thumb to consider when selecting your clothing is to consider being slightly dressier than you would at home. Americans tend to be much more casual and dressed down than the rest of the world. By dressing up a little more than you normally would at home, you are more likely to fit in with locals in your everyday activities. The concept of wearing sports clothing to school or business casual clothing to work is not practiced in many other areas of the world. For example, while your typical winter school outfit might be a hoodie sweatshirt and a pair of leggings or sweatpants, that outfit can look out of place in many foreign universities. Likewise, in your job in the United States you may feel perfectly normal wearing jeans to your office, but in other countries, jeans may be seen as inappropriate. This does not mean that your clothing needs to be expensive or that you have to wear suits or fancy dresses every day. Instead, consider clothing that looks a bit more polished or slightly more fitted to your body. If we take the example of the school outfit, try swapping the hoodie for a sweater, and the leggings or sweatpants for jeans or other trousers. If you will be working abroad, we recommend checking with your employer for any employee attire guidelines or information about how most people dress for the office. In general, though, dressing slightly nicer than business casual is usually acceptable for most foreign offices. This could mean wearing slacks instead of jeans or wearing a button-down shirt or blouse instead of a t-shirt-style top. Naturally, you can still have casual clothing for activities that are more physically active or for sports and working out. Let's say you are going for a forest walk, in that case, people will expect you to wear athletic clothing, not slacks and dress shoes. For other activities though, you might want to consider bringing at least one dressier outfit. You might be invited to a special event, and you will likely want to have something with you already rather than trying to shop for a special occasion on the fly.

Along with your clothing, you will want to consider your footwear carefully. The most important rule for footwear when going abroad is comfort. In many other countries, walking and using public transportation is more common, especially for study abroad students. Unlike US institutions, many foreign universities do not have on-site housing. This means you will probably be walking several blocks or taking some form of public transit to get to your classes. If you are in a mid-size to large city, prepare for that public transit to be crowded where you may be expected to stand while traveling. Similarly, if you are going abroad to work, chances are you too will be taking public transportation rather than driving at first in your new country. If you are traveling to a historic area, consider that the walking surfaces may be made of historic materials such as cobblestones. While your favorite pair of heeled sandals might seem comfortable walking on a smoothly paved surface, they might feel very different walking across a historic street with all the wear and tear of the years. Additionally, consider that close-toed shoes are preferable in cities to open-toed shoes and sandals. Cities in general tend to be dirtier than you realize (also true in the United States) and you may find yourself with very dirty feet in your sandals even after just a few hours of walking around. If you are going abroad to work, as with your clothing, you will want to have some dressier shoes that are still comfortable so that they coordinate well with your outfit. Although tennis shoes might be considered business casual in the United States, they will likely look out of place in most foreign offices. Remember too that you will want to have at least one pair of dressier shoes that go with your special occasion outfit.

While abroad you might also want to shop at local stores for clothing or shoes. Be aware that sizing can be very different between countries and often the numerical systems that are used for both clothes and shoes are vastly different from those of the United States. Consider the example size table for women's clothing with sizing numbers from different countries.

It helps to know your measurements in centimeters to find the proper sizes as almost all other countries use the metric system for measuring clothing. Also do not be surprised if a store sales clerk measures you in the store to find out your proper size. If you are in a size range that is considered outside of the standard or straight sizing, we recommend researching clothing stores for your destination so that you will know ahead of time some possible shopping options for you. Similar to here in the United States, it helps to have a good idea of the stores that carry your sizes before you arrive. Even if you don't plan on doing much clothing shopping while abroad, you will want to have this information at the ready in case you do need new things (e.g., lost luggage,

Table 3.1

Country	Size Small	Size Medium	Size Large
U.S.	6	8	10
U.K.	8	10	12
France	36	38	40
Germany	34	36	38
Italy	40	42	44
Japan	9	11	13
Australian/NZ	10	12	14

ruined by washer, or stolen bag). Fortunately, today, there are more people online who provide advice for petite, plus-sized, big and tall, and other nonstandard-sized shopping in other countries. You can find these people through blogs, fashion sites, and social media sites typically. We also suggest checking the availability of online retailers such as Amazon while you are abroad. For example, many people can use their Amazon account while abroad and have packages delivered to their international address. This will of course depend on your destination, but it can be a good option for shopping if you cannot find what you need in local stores.

ELECTRONICS AND PERSONAL ITEMS

As with your clothing and accessories, you should decide which electronics and personal items are essential, which would be nice to take if you have room, and which could be left at home. Especially in the case of personal items that you buy regularly, like shampoo, you might consider purchasing them at your destination instead of hauling them with you. For other items, particularly electronics, consider their portability, usefulness, and replacement cost. Larger or bulkier items can be difficult to pack, and you may discover that trying to bring them with you is not worth it. Likewise, with anything that has a very high replacement cost, it may not be worth the risk of damaging or losing the item during your travels.

With any of your electronic devices, you must first consider the type of power used in that country. For many international countries, the type of power is different than in the United States and will require you to have a power converter. Also, you should know that power can vary from country to country even in the same general region, so make sure you have researched your country and any countries you may visit during your stay. Be sure to purchase a power converter in the United States before departing for your destination country. We recommend purchasing at least two converters in case one does not work or blows a fuse when you arrive. Power converters are not always easy to find in other countries and without one you might end up having a useless electronic device with you. Also, be aware of the difference between a power converter, which changes the voltage from the power source to match that of your device, and a power adapter, which only changes the shape of the plug. To be on the safe side, using a power converter for each of your devices is a better choice to help ensure that your devices will still work while abroad.

When traveling with a laptop or tablet, there are a few aspects to keep in mind. First, consider what type of case or protective traveling gear you may need. At home, you might be used to carrying your laptop around in your backpack or bag without any additional protection, but this might not be sufficient when traveling abroad. If you consider the various types of transportation you are likely to use while traveling, you might find that it would be better to find a more protective type of bag or gear to keep your laptop or tablet from getting damaged. Another thought to keep in mind is that people in other countries might not use their laptops and tablets in as many public areas as we do in the United States. While some locations might be fairly universal for laptop use, such as libraries, they might not be welcome in some areas that you traditionally find to be laptop-acceptable. Let's consider a coffee shop. In the United States, almost all coffee shops are welcoming to laptops, and you can buy one coffee and spend hours working there on your laptop. However, this can vary greatly in other areas, even in the same city. In Paris, some cafés are welcoming to laptops and do not expect you to make more than your initial purchase of a coffee. Other cafés may expect you to continue to make purchases, including something more substantial, such as lunch if you will be staying for several hours. Sometimes these cafés have designated laptop hours or days when you are permitted to use them. Finally, other cafés have banned laptops altogether and will tell you to either put the laptop away or leave. Tablets are generally more acceptable in public spaces, but even they have been banned from some places.

Remember too that using technology in a public area may also be an issue of safety. While it might be fine to have your laptop or tablet in your bag as you take public transportation, you may want to keep from advertising that you have such an expensive device with you. Reading your iPad on the bus might feel normal and like a good use of your time, but it might bring the attention of a pickpocket riding on that same bus. Additionally, using your devices in public, especially on public transportation, takes your attention away from your surroundings. Sitting in a place like a library or café where others are doing the same is fine. However, while on public transportation it is a good idea to remain more aware of your surroundings. Along these same lines, you should never leave your things unattended even if you ask someone to watch them or if you'll "just be a moment." We would never do this in the United States, but we know that in some areas people are more trusting and it can be a common occurrence, especially on college campuses.

As with your laptop or tablet, you will want to think about preparations for traveling with your phone. The first step here is to contact your phone service provider and ask about international options for using your phone to make calls, send messages, and use the internet while abroad. In many cases you will need to authorize an international plan before going abroad. Also, please be aware that if you are on a family phone plan, the primary person on the account must be the one to authorize this. The international plan provided by your phone company may be very expensive and not ideal for long-term use. Therefore, you will most likely want to purchase a new SIM card for local use. For your phone to use the new SIM card, however, it must be unlocked. Again, you will need to check with your phone service provider to determine if your phone is or is not unlocked. Many international phone service providers have pay-as-you-go options and are the better choice for you instead of a contract. Usually, you can visit a phone service provider store to purchase your new SIM card. In some instances, you might even see them being sold at special vending machines or electronic kiosks in the airport or the downtown area of major cities. With the new SIM card, you will have a local phone number that you can share with friends and family to use while you are abroad. Nevertheless, most people end up using the available data that they purchase with the SIM to use other apps for communication rather than the standard phone call and SMS text messaging apps. The reason for this is that phone calls and standard texting can be very expensive and will use up your pay-as-you-go credits very quickly. It also saves your family and friends from the expense of international calling and texting. At the time of this writing, the most popular communication app abroad is WhatsApp which provides text messaging, phone calling, and video calling and uses data or Wi-Fi. You can set it up with your US phone number to make it easy for your American family and friends to find your account. You will also find that most local friends and acquaintances that you meet abroad will primarily use WhatsApp as their most common way to communicate. Other popular communication apps that use data or Wi-Fi include Instagram, Facebook Messenger, Google Meet, Google Chat, Discord, and SnapChat.

As with your other electronics, you should have a sturdy case for your phone and a screen protector to help it stand up to the rigors of international travel. Cobblestone streets can pack quite a wallop if you drop your phone on them! You will also want to be more conscious of where you keep your phone when not using it. Many people are accustomed to keeping their phones in a back pocket, but this is often not secure enough, especially in crowded areas or on public transportation. (Please note the same is true for keeping wallets and other valuables in your back pockets.) We recommend carrying your phone in a front pocket or secured in a bag. Sometimes Americans worry that their phones might be too flashy or too nice and they are worried about bringing them abroad. If that is the case for you, you can always pick up a less expensive used phone or an older model before going abroad. However, you will likely find that locals are using the same types of phones as you, with many people having the latest models, especially in major cities around the globe. Usually, it is the ease of access to your phone that leads to it being pickpocketed more than the brand or model. Before leaving for your destination, it is a good idea to know about your avenues for getting a replacement phone should it be necessary. It is also a very good idea to make sure you have important information backed up to a data storage cloud so you won't lose all your fantastic travel photos or your crucial work documents should something happen to your phone (or other devices).

For other personal items, the major ones to consider are any that are related to your health and personal care. If you take medication, you will need to make sure you have access to that medication while abroad. In many instances this means bringing prescription medication with you. Generally, you will need to contact your health insurance provider several weeks before your trip so that they can authorize your pharmacy to provide you with more of your medication than normal. If the medication that you take is particularly expensive or uncommon, you might need to contact your insurance provider even earlier to give sufficient time for approval. It is also a good idea to have a record of all your medications from your doctor's office so that you can provide proof that they are your prescriptions. Depending on your destination, some medications may be purchased over the counter while abroad, while others that are purchased over the counter here might require prescriptions. Make sure you investigate this before you go so you can be certain that you will have the medicines that you need. As a reminder, your prescription medications need to go into your carry-on luggage and should never be put into checked baggage.

One thing to consider for your health needs is any menstrual supplies that you need. While those supplies can be purchased abroad, they might be different from the ones that you are used to having at home. Many people find they can make the shift to foreign products, but others choose to have a supply of their preferred brand with them. You should investigate if your preferred brand is sold in other countries because if it is from a large company there is a chance it can be found in your abroad location (sometimes it is sold under a different name but is the same brand). However, keep in mind that even if your brand is sold there, the product itself may not be exactly like the one sold at home. You should remember this for any other personal care products that you need, especially those brands that might be difficult to find in other countries.

WHAT TO LEAVE HOME

In helping you decide what to leave at home, we recommend asking yourself three questions about your items: What will it cost to replace this item? Is this item essential to my day-to-day life? Is this item available in my destination country? Using that as your system of elimination you can leave behind anything that would be too costly to lose or anything that will take up the valuable space in your suitcase and/or living accommodations.

One of the first things we suggest leaving at home is any unnecessary electronics. Items such as a bulky hairdryer, a gaming system, or a smart speaker, should be left at home. For some electronics, such as hairdryers or other hair styling tools, you might be provided with them in your living accommodations or be able to purchase new ones at a reasonable price in your new country. Sometimes there are even ones that you can borrow from a study abroad office or international student office. (Also, as a bonus you don't have to worry about overloading your US devices with the different electric current.) For other devices, you may simply need to take a break from using them during your time abroad. Think about trying other methods to fulfill the needs of that device, such as using headphones instead of a smart speaker, or spending your time in other ways as you explore your new home.

An easy way to save on space in your suitcase is to leave most toiletries at home and purchase new ones to use when you arrive at your destination. You will likely want to bring a few small-sized items to get you through the first few days, but it is a good idea to leave the larger bottles and packages at home. This will also help from any unexpected leaks or bottle explosions in your suitcase during transit. It's not fun to have to immediately do an entire load of laundry because your sunscreen has opened and coated all your clothing! Unless you are going to a very remote area, you should find your necessary toiletries in your new country. You may even discover new international brands and products that you love too. For example, if you are traveling to South Korea, you will find that Korean skincare is known to be both affordable and highly effective.

Another set of items to leave at home are those that are very expensive. Traveling abroad is not usually the best time to wear your priciest jewelry, costly shoes, or designer backpack. First, expensive items can bring unwanted attention to you and make you a target for thieves. Pickpockets are common in large cities, especially in tourist areas. People who look like they have money are usually targeted first. Additionally, while nice, many expensive items may not be as durable for international travel. The exclusive sneakers you love might not look so great after walking around all day in a historic city or a trek through a nature preserve. It is better to have cheaper alternative items that will still be useful. For example, if you are used to wearing a smartwatch, consider getting an inexpensive digital watch to wear while you travel. While other less expensive items could still be lost, stolen, or ruined, it will not feel as bad to lose a $25 ring as compared to a $2,500 one.

Finally, anything irreplaceable should be left at home in the care of someone you trust. There is no need to risk losing or damaging an item such as that by bringing it with you during your travels. If it's something very important to you, you might consider taking a photo of it and bringing the photo with you as a way to have the item with you in spirit.

PACKING LISTS

To help you out with your packing, we include the following packing lists. Please note these lists are rather generic and gender-neutral to give you a place to start, but you will want to tailor them to suit your needs. Keep in mind our first rule though—you need less than you think!

Clothing

- five school or business attire bottoms (pants, skirts)
- three casual attire bottoms (pants, skirts, shorts)
- five school or business attire tops (shirts, blouses, sweaters)
- three casual attire tops (t-shirts, casual shirts)
- one dressier outfit
- underwear for nine days
- socks or hosiery for nine days
- two pairs of comfortable shoes (suitable for school or business)
- two nights of sleepwear
- swimsuit
- lightweight jacket
- accessories
- glasses and contacts
- sunglasses
- scarf (one that could double as a shawl is very useful)
- tote bag (good for daily use or grocery shopping)

Travel Clothing

- comfortable bottoms (preferably with some stretch)
- short-sleeve top
- jacket or cardigan
- comfortable underwear (women may want to consider a wire-free bra for their flight)
- compression socks (ideal for a long-haul flight; will help your legs feel better and increase circulation)
- comfortable shoes (wear your heaviest ones on the plane to keep them out of your luggage)
- coat (if traveling during the winter)

Travel Documents and Wallet Items

- passport
- secondary ID
- medical insurance cards
- credit card
- cash
- vaccination certification

Electronics

- two power converters
- cell phone
- cell phone charger
- laptop or tablet
- laptop or tablet charger
- portable rechargeable power bank (backup battery)

Personal Care

- travel-sized toiletries
- toothbrush
- hairbrush or comb
- cosmetics
- personal products
- Band-aids
- pain reliever
- stomach medication
- prescription medications

Miscellaneous

- journal
- travel pillow
- earplugs
- sleep mask

CHAPTER 4

Culture Shock

HAVE YOU EVER GONE TO A PART OF THE UNITED STATES THAT may even be a short distance away from your home and been quite surprised about something you encountered? Say you are from a large city like New York City and you travel to a rural area in the Plains, or vice versa. Chances are you are going to be quite surprised about some component of how people live in the place you are visiting, even if you feel you have seen a lot of it on TV or in movies. This "surprise" is a type of culture shock, when you have some kind of emotional reaction to a cultural difference you encounter in a culture. In this chapter, we will dive deep into what culture shock is and how it affects your study abroad experiences. Importantly, when discussing cultural differences in any way, it can be very easy to treat communities' cultures as monolithic, meaning everyone acts the same way all the time. This is very much not the case. Even in places where one cultural practice is prevalent, there will always be people who don't practice it or don't practice it in the "popular" way. Keep this in mind as you read this chapter, prepare to study abroad, and experience your host culture.

WHAT IS CULTURE SHOCK?
One of the pioneer definitions of culture shock comes from the field of anthropology, indicating that culture shock is the anxiety

that comes about when someone loses "familiar signs and symbols of social intercourse."[1] This means that whatever differences you may encounter during your time abroad may provoke a type of emotional reaction. You may be surprised when you see people dipping their French fries in mayonnaise or when you see a protest fighting for labor rights because you may not be accustomed to these sights in your home community. This is normal! Importantly, even though words like "anxiety" and "shock," along with some of the descriptions below carry negative connotations, culture shock doesn't have to be a bad thing. Being exposed to a new cultural practice can lead you to think differently about an issue and perhaps even understand it better.

Although everyone will experience culture shock in their own way in reaction to their combination of cultural practices, for most people, culture shock is a cyclical phenomenon.[2] This means that you will pass through certain stages of culture shock. Even within each stage of the cycle, you may find that one day you'll feel better about your host country's culture while other days you may see it a little bit more negatively. That's ok! This is normal. When you arrive in your host country, you will likely be very excited about living in new surroundings. Everything different is new and exciting. This is labeled as a honeymoon period, when you may feel extreme positivity toward your host country. At some point, you will start transitioning to a stage when you can notice cultural differences better. In this stage, you may notice things you don't like, perhaps even feel sadness, anxiety, or distress about your study abroad situation. Typically, this stage transitions into one of adjustment, especially once you're feeling more familiar with your new surroundings, and adaptation when you have begun to accept the cultural difference.

Let's take a look at these steps in the context of an example. In this example, you arrive in your host country where English is not a primary language and where you don't have reliable internet access and, therefore, less connection to life in the United States.

On your first day, you realize that American TV shows appear on TV in your host country but the dialogue is dubbed into the local language. At first, you think it is amazing and very interesting that you can watch *Friends* in a different language (honeymoon stage). After some time, this excitement wears off and you become very annoyed with the fact that your favorite characters don't sound like they do in the United States (transition). Therefore, you boycott watching American TV if you can't do it in what you see as an authentic way. Your host family, however, doesn't see watching dubbed episodes of *Friends* as inauthentic so they continue to watch them. Over time, you become more familiar with watching in a different language and you ultimately sit down and enjoy the show in what is a normal way in your host country (adjustment and adaptation).

How Will You See Culture Shock during Study Abroad?

You will likely experience culture shock in numerous contexts during study abroad. While there is no way for us to predict the exact ways you will experience culture shock because that will depend on how you perceive your home cultures, your host cultures, and the relative distance between those cultures, we have chosen some common types of culture shock. In addition, we give some recommendations for approaching any potential issues in each of the categories.

Food

Food may not seem like the most important part about immersing yourself in a new culture but it is one of the first ways that many people experience culture shock. Think about it. We all will eat pretty quickly after stepping off the plane in our host countries. You may be surprised about how to get your food, how it's prepared, how new flavors are used and combined, and more. One of the biggest shocks for some people involves differing practices

related to food and drink. Let's take the example of vegetarianism.
If you are a vegetarian, you may find interpretations of the concept
that are different than what you are familiar with, including even
more vegetable-based options. You may encounter people who
accept that you are a vegetarian but then assume that you eat fish.
Despite what the specifics of your culture shock are, you are likely
to feel some kind of anxiety (transition stage) as you figure out
how to adjust and adapt to the vegetarian practices of your new
environment. If you find yourself in a culture where vegetarian
practices are pleasing to you, you may even have a honeymoon
period!

The most common food-related culture shocks involve something a person doesn't like or believes that they won't like. First, if
your personal beliefs and health permit it, try everything with an
authentic effort. You may like the new food! If you don't, you can
likely find a way to avoid eating it again. If what you are being
offered will hurt you physically or violate an important belief for
you, you need to make an effort to find a culturally appropriate
substitute, that is healthy for you, and allows you to still participate in your host culture.

If you are traveling with a restrictive diet, be sure to do plenty
of preparation and research on the availability of the foods you
need before you go abroad. This might mean learning new words
and phrases that are not typically taught to you in a standard language course. This will also mean scoping out which markets and
restaurants might have the food you need. Additionally, a specialized website or community may exist to help you navigate your
diet while traveling. For example, for people with celiac disease or
who have gluten intolerance, the website Wheatless Wanderlust
can help you manage your gluten-free diet while abroad.[3] Nonetheless, you will need to prepare yourself for things to be different
and you should be ready for times when you cannot find the exact
food item you are used to getting at home.

Interactions with Other People

After you've had a meal, you are likely to begin noticing how people interact in your host country, some of which may be different than what you're used to and may provoke some culture shock. By interactions with other people, we are referring to several things. Let's explore some of them here. You may notice cultural practices relating to greetings quickly. Many times in the United States, a greeting may involve a handshake, a hug if you are close, or just a verbal greeting without any touching. This is different in many places. For example, in much of Latin America, it is normal for people to give each other a quick kiss on the left cheek when they see each other. In other places, there may be two kisses on either cheek. Knowing when to do this can involve observing the intimacy of the relationships, the genders of the participants, and their surroundings. You may also find that the ways people interact with members of their families and their friends may be different. They may spend more time with their families and less time with their friends than you are accustomed to, or vice versa. It is also quite possible that you notice strangers acting differently with each other. For example, if you smile or say hello to someone walking on the street or attempt to converse with a server at a restaurant like you would at home, they may think that's weird because they don't know you. It's not that they are mean or antisocial. It's just that they don't know you and it's not normal for them to talk to strangers. For Josh, these service interactions were the hardest to adjust to because he had worked in a large retail store for several years before going abroad. He was used to having small talk with customers but he also didn't always want to do that. He saw the value of a service interaction abroad that centered only on the transaction at hand.

A key concept to consider when experiencing interaction with people from another country is standards of politeness. You may already recognize that politeness can vary greatly from place to place even within the United States. This is also true in other countries. Just as other practices are different, politeness and manners can be very different in other countries. The important aspect to understand here is that it will take time and observation to understand how politeness is carried out. In some ways, you may find that you are being overly polite to the point where people may think you are insincere. In other ways, you may wonder why everyone seems to be acting so rude toward you. In many cases, these are simply differences with politeness norms across cultures and are not necessarily people being rude to you on purpose. For example, when traveling to Taiwan, Melanie found it surprising how many times people said "thank you" during an interaction. It was often repeated multiple times in a service conversation, almost to the point of feeling silly to her US standards. However, when traveling to Mexico, she found the opposite, that people rarely said "thank you" for things and that she often stuck out for saying it too much.

So, what do you do when you encounter new types of social interaction? Unlike in our recommendations about food, where we said to try it once and not to repeat it if you don't like it, you should do all you can to accommodate to how local people interact. This is going to help you integrate yourself the best. This may mean learning the particulars of how to give and accept a greeting kiss or practice politeness. You could need to learn to not expect small talk with people you don't know, or the opposite. In this case, don't rely on your restaurant servers for your interactions. Lean into the people you know better like your host family, classmates, or other local people you have met.

Social Norms
In all cultures, there are certain societal norms that a large part of the population prescribes. This is part of what makes them a distinct culture because it means they share many of the same beliefs and values. These norms can include anything from religion (how, when, and where the faith is practiced), gender (roles for men and

women; clothing), race and ethnicity (treated equally or differently), and many more. This can even include something like who you should tip and how much. It's important to recognize that you are arriving in your host country with a set of social norms in your mind that are based on the cultures you have grown up in and they may be quite different from what you observe in your host country. For example, you may come from a community where it is normal for both men and women to work outside of the house in the same types of jobs but you end up studying abroad in a place where women face many more barriers regarding what types of jobs they have or even if they are allowed to work.

For some of these social norms, it may be pretty easy to go through the culture shock cycle and accept that, for instance, it's normal to eat lunch at 2:00 p.m. rather than at noon. You just learn to eat a 10:00 a.m. snack, adjust, and accept. However, there are other differences in social norms that you may find strongly go against your personal beliefs and values. You may not be able to adjust and accept but you must be the one to critically evaluate these differences and decide that you are not going to participate. Do recall, though, that adjustment to and acceptance of a cultural difference does not mean that you have to participate. For example, if you perceive that most people in your host community don't seem to practice religion in the way you do and it's important for you to continue your practices, you should do some research to figure out how you can practice your faith. You may find a faith community that is similar to what you have at home even if they are much smaller than you're accustomed to. In cases like this, it can help to be reasonably flexible. Perhaps that faith community doesn't align perfectly with your beliefs but if they're close, it may be worth joining them.

Social Life
Let's say you're coming from somewhere where your university's residential campus is the center of all social life. You may live, eat,

study, work, compete, and socialize on campus with people in that community. This is normal in many universities in the United States. The university where Josh teaches is just like that for many students. That is one of the reasons students choose to attend that small rural university. However, when you go abroad, you may find that local university students do not center their social lives around the university campus. There may not be an actual campus as you know it since the university may be comprised of buildings sprinkled throughout a city. Social lives may vary from country to country and community to community based on who is included, what they do together, and when and where they hang out. In some places, you may find that social lives are centered around families, childhood friends, or members of other groups (e.g., religious groups, teams). What people do and when and where they do activities may also differ. While you may be accustomed to having coffee on campus with someone who lives in your residence hall at 8 p.m., you may find it's much more normal to have a beer with a long-time friend at 10 p.m. (or much later) in a bar.

Since much of the success of a study abroad experience can be based on social interaction, it will be important for you to observe and adapt to the norms of your host community's social life, at least to some extent. This will especially be the case if the majority of people in the host community observe some kind of practice that affects social life, such as eating meals with family. If certain meals are always taken with family members for the majority of people, you can't expect them to hang out with you during those times. Instead, talk with them about times that they would normally hang out with friends, find a mutually agreeable time, and meet with them even if it's at a different time than you normally would socialize. For example, even though Josh likes to eat dinner earlier than many people in Spain (when he's not with other people), he adapts and eats later because many times people he knows in Spain eat dinner with family later and are more likely to be free for a drink with him at around 6 p.m. For another example, Melanie's students who have studied in Japan were surprised to learn how late people went to clubs and bars. At home in the United States, they were used to going out around 9:30 or 10 p.m., but in Japan, they found that most places didn't get going until after midnight and that it wasn't unusual to be out until 5 or 6 a.m.

Language

For many people, one of the biggest challenges associated with study abroad is language, whether or not you are studying language formally or not. Some people may even find that it's hard to communicate in places where English is used widely. The reason why this is a major challenge for a lot of people is that we are very accustomed to having little to no trouble communicating whatever message we want to convey in our home communities. However, when you arrive in your host country, you will likely encounter a language barrier quickly, perhaps even on day one. Even though Josh already had an undergraduate degree in Spanish when he started his year abroad, he had a hard time communicating with people to figure out how to get from the airport to his hotel. Similarly, after spending five months in Spain, Melanie thought it would be so nice to travel to Scotland where everything was in English. Yet when she arrived, she found the Scottish accent so difficult to understand that she quickly wished she was back in Spain!

Let's take a look at how language can follow the culture shock cycle. First, in your honeymoon phase, you may be feeling pretty proud of your language skills once you get the swing of navigating daily interactions such as meals with your host family and ordering a beverage. As time and experiences accumulate, you may lose confidence. This may happen due to difficult academics or the need to interact in contexts you haven't encountered. Finally, your adjustment and acceptance of cultural (and linguistic) differences may appear once you realize that you are not expected to be able to communicate in all contexts. It's normal to be highly proficient in your second language but still not be able to speak about some topics. For example, in 2023, Josh traveled to Spain with his parents. Even though he had been a Spanish speaker for nearly twenty-five years, he needed to quickly learn vocabulary about quilting when his mother wanted to go to quilt shops. He didn't see this as a deficit in skills but knew he needed to look up some words because he had never talked about quilting in Spanish.

What should you do when encountering culture shock related to language? No matter your proficiencies in your host language, the best thing you can do is to learn some language. Even if you know zero words, start using an app or begin a language course. Once you know how to greet people and introduce yourself, start using that language in the street. Keep going with phrases you find yourself needing frequently. Doing this will make the language less foreign and will help you adjust and accept any language barriers. In addition, you should work to improve your ability to live in ambiguity, meaning that you don't know everything that is going on or being said around you. You may be very uncomfortable with this but it is a crucial perspective to adopt when you are studying abroad in a place where you aren't a native speaker of a host language. If you find yourself feeling anxious in these situations, take a beat and remind yourself that they are almost certainly not talking about you and that you are fine with not knowing what they are talking about.

Academics

If you are taking courses abroad, you are probably thinking quite a bit about the courses you will take. What these courses look like will depend on the type of program you are going with, your course of study, your host country, among other reasons. No matter the program, there will be something different than what you are used to at home. Some examples of culture shock that you may experience in academia may include teaching methods. Your professor may rely on lectures while you are used to reading and group work. The relationship between student and professor may differ, as well, especially if the class is of a size that is new to you. Speaking of relationships, you may find that local students utilize the university differently than you do at your home institution. They may come, go to class, work for a bit, and go home, without socializing much. Even though all of these could cause culture shock, one of the biggest academic shocks could come at the end of the semester if you are in a place where final course grades are posted publicly. In the United States, the Family Educational Rights and Privacy Act (FERPA) prohibits a university from displaying your personal information like this. However, recall that you are in a different country under that country's legal jurisdiction, as we mentioned in chapter 2. If allowed by law, policy, and custom, you may find out your course grade just like other people would find out your course grade: posted in a hallway.

It should make sense that you would experience academic culture shock in ways that correspond to the issue. For instance, you may have an easy time adjusting and accepting a new teaching method, especially if you find it effective. However, some issues, such as grading, may be harder to work through. What do you do if you're experiencing academic culture shock? First, even though you are abroad, you are still not alone. If you are having a cultural problem with a class or a professor, you should meet with someone you trust who also works with study abroad. This can be your host country administrator, your home institution's study abroad office, a local classmate, or even the professor. They can help you determine if you are experiencing culture shock that can be overcome or if your problem deserves extra attention. They can even help you figure out how to work with faculty or course structure.

A note about communicating with foreign professors is warranted here. In many countries, the relationship between professors and students is much more formal. While foreign professors will typically have office hours that are designed to provide you with an opportunity to meet with them, they may not have the relaxed and conversational atmosphere of office hours with many US professors. Remember too that it is best to ask questions that can help you be more successful, rather than questions that can sound like critiques. For example, if your professor does not grade assignments quickly you might say, "I was hoping to check with you on my progress in the course. Is there anything you feel I could be doing better?" rather than, "Do you know when you'll get our papers graded? I really want to know my grade so I know how I'm doing."

Living Situations
Housing may look quite different in your host country. Such differences may pertain to size, amenities, style, use, and even who lives there. For many Americans, the first thing they notice about housing in much of the rest of the world is that it is smaller than in the United States. This is more likely to be your case than the opposite where your housing is larger than a typical American home. (Note, this may even affect the way you pack since you may not have as much closet space as you do at home!) In addition to being smaller, there may be more people living there. If you are living with a host family, you may live with adult children or elderly grandparents, depending on the customs and economics of the host country. The place you live may have different amenities that you're not accustomed to. The home, or the people who live there, may have things you haven't seen such as kitchen utensils and appliances (elaborate rice cookers, unique cookware, and food) and maybe even bidets in bathrooms. There may also be things you will have to get used to not having, such as clothes dryers, air conditioning, and perhaps reliable internet and electricity. In much of the world, power and water are very expensive. This leads to changes in how people use their houses. Shorter, less frequent showers help keep the water bill down while limiting the number of lights, and climate control in use can lower the electricity bill.

Finally, the style of your living situation may be unfamiliar to you. For example, if you grew up in an urban apartment building in the United States, living in a single-family house in your host country may bring surprises.

Where you live will likely cause some type of culture shock since there are so many factors that make up your situation. Let's continue with the previous example of the urbanite who grew up in an apartment building and lived on campus in a residence hall after that. They go from their home to a single-family house in rural Ireland. They may experience a honeymoon period in which they relish the peace and tranquility that comes with not living around many other people. However, they learn that it is also harder to get services and goods since you have to travel longer distances to get them (transition). Eventually, they figure out their new routine and move on (adjustment and acceptance). Whatever your case may be, we urge you to practice open-mindedness and flexibility as you work through the culture shock cycle, especially since reacting negatively to how your hosts live can be quite insulting. Instead of outwardly reacting with negativity, ask questions to learn more about the ways they live.

Reverse Culture Shock

Even though we will approach reverse culture shock more in chapter 9, it is a concept that is worth mentioning in this chapter. Reverse culture shock is like the culture shock that we have been describing in this chapter except that it involves your return to your home culture rather than your arrival to your host culture. Before you go abroad, and even before you leave to return home, you may not realize that reverse culture shock will happen. But it will in some way. So, what does it look like? It will involve your reaction to a cultural concept that you encounter at home and you will go through some form of honeymoon, transition, adjustment, and acceptance cycle. Just like with culture shock, this can be related to things like worldview, food, or social life, among others.

It's important to note that reverse culture shock is normal and doesn't mean that you hate your home culture now that you've lived outside of it. It just means that you have changed and your perspectives have changed. Check out chapter 9 for more information about what those changes may be and how they can affect how you see your home culture.

After reading and thinking about culture shock, you may be feeling pretty intimidated by study abroad. Our hope for this chapter is to give you some insight into what types of differences you may encounter and some ways to process them. There is no way we can include all possible cultural differences in all possible communities but if you keep these general tips in mind, you will be better prepared to get the most out of your time abroad.

CHAPTER 5

Goals and Strategies

As you are organizing your trip abroad, it will be very easy to focus on planning for tangible elements like packing or arranging your travel documents. Nonetheless, we highly recommend that you spend time considering the goals you have for your stay abroad. We see this as a key part of your pre-departure activities that will help you get the very most out of your travels. The excitement of planning for such a large trip can be overwhelming. At times, you may find yourself struggling to concentrate on all the details, especially as you get closer to your departure date. If you can set aside some time before you leave to think about your goals, you will feel more focused and ready for your trip.

Goal setting will also help organize your time while abroad. Whether you are planning a stay of three weeks or a stay of four months, there will be less time abroad than it initially seems. Setting clear goals for what you want to achieve from the trip allows you to prioritize your activities and can help you stay focused on doing the things that you intend to do. Having these goals will also help you get through the initial sensation of wanting to do everything and anything you can while abroad. While that feeling is normal, you will soon realize that if you do not have a plan for your time, you may end up getting distracted from activities that you originally wanted to do.

In this chapter, we offer ideas about setting cultural goals, social goals, linguistic goals, touristic goals, and academic goals. While this is not an exhaustive list of goal categories, we feel these give you a good jumping-off point for your pre-departure planning. We recommend writing down your goals as you read this chapter. Additionally, to help you achieve your goals, we also provide various strategies, which suggest different methods that we know to be effective.

CULTURAL GOALS AND STRATEGIES

If you have decided to travel abroad, chances are you are doing so for some kind of cultural reason. You may have said to yourself, "I am studying abroad because I want to immerse myself in the culture." But what is *the* culture of your host community? Delving into different parts of culture can affect how you state and accomplish your cultural goals.

Big C Culture

Big C culture refers to things like art, architecture, food, and any other aspect of culture that is obvious, or quite visible when you are visiting a community. It is normal to want to learn and experience these types of cultures, and it is usually quite easy to do so by going to museums and restaurants and exploring a city.

Small c Culture

As opposed to Big C culture, Small c culture refers to the daily life of the community, and the ways people live, which may be less apparent to a visitor. It will be more difficult to become immersed into this type of culture because it will require the fostering of personal relationships with local people to learn about social norms regarding promptness or behaviors at meals, for example.

Understanding the differences between different types of cultures will help you decide what your goals are and how you should go about them. If you truly want to learn about daily life and become integrated into the related practices, you will want to employ different strategies than if you want to learn about art. You will need to seek out interpersonal interactions with local people. In the next sections, you will see that this may be difficult. Therefore, you should put effort into your social interactions.

SOCIAL GOALS AND STRATEGIES

Setting clear social goals is important so that you maximize your chances of meeting potential friends and enhance the quality of your social interactions while abroad. In this section, you'll learn about the types of social situations you can aspire to be a part of. Two clear threads that you may notice throughout the section are that you should (a) do what you do at home to meet friends and (b) be extremely deliberate about how you go about doing so.

Homestays and Roommates

In nearly all study abroad programs, students live with someone else. As mentioned in chapter 1, typically, these people fall into three categories: host families, local roommates, and roommates from other countries, including the student's home country. Common sense may dictate that the people you live with may be the best source of social interaction. However, this may not be the case. Consider the roommates you may have had in your home community. They were probably just as busy as you are so it may have been hard to interact. A roommate situation during study abroad may be similar.

Homestays may be a more reliable strategy to have social interaction in the place you stay during study abroad. In many programs, the host family is expected, or may actually be contractually obligated, to socialize with students living with them. Frequently, such interactions occur over meals and in the company of other family members. Thus, this living situation offers the chance to accomplish a social goal while also providing you with a way to experience the daily life of a local family.

Conversation Partners

Many study abroad providers, particularly those that offer language instruction, facilitate conversation partners so that students have the opportunity to meet and interact with someone local. In some programs, these interactions occur in groups while in others they may be one-on-one. These interactions frequently involve a cultural and/or linguistic exchange. Each person has the opportunity to learn about the other's culture and, in many cases, practice the other's native languages. With luck, these conversation partners can become true friendships. If you choose to use this strategy to be social, we encourage you to be open to a wide variety of possibilities. For example, when Josh studied abroad at age twenty-three, he ended up with a forty-year-old conversation partner who became one of his best friends in Spain.

"Typical" Social Groups

In many cases, activities that you do at home will also be available in your host country. These may include sports, arts, or religion, for example. If you participate in a religious organization at home, it may be a good idea to search for a similar organization during study abroad. Similarly, if you like to sing in choirs, seek out a choir that may accept you. You will probably have a lot of overlapping interests with the people in those situations, making it easier to foster relationships.

Meeting Local People during Study Abroad

It can be frustratingly difficult to meet local people during study abroad. This is not because locals are unfriendly or do not like to be around foreigners. On the contrary, they may be as interested in you and your experiences as you are in theirs. However, two points are working against a meaningful relationship. First, it is hard to build friendships in adulthood when people have numerous obligations to pay attention to. Second, the temporary nature of study abroad means that the friendship may be temporary. If you are studying abroad in a place with lots of international students, that local friend may have already gone through cycles of making international friends and losing them. This discourages them from putting effort into meeting new international friends. Given these challenges, it is not realistic to anticipate meeting a large number of local friends. Instead, plan to meet one or two people outside of your living situation with whom you forge a friendship at some level. It is important to recognize that it is hard to create strong social bonds during study abroad given personal obligations on all sides and how temporary everyone knows the study abroad experience is. These challenges necessitate a change of perspective from one that you may have at your home institution. To make things easier for yourself, try an activity that is unique and culturally relevant in your host country and that many local people participate in. For example, if you are studying abroad in the Alps, you could join a local ski club.

Friends from Your Study Abroad Cohort
In cases in which you study abroad alongside a group of students from your home country, it can be easy and comforting to form close social bonds with those students. This makes sense when you consider that these students are experiencing similar events, emotions, and personal revelations given their similar experiences abroad. Many students who are studying abroad share a lot of qualities and goals, making them naturally flock toward each other. They can also be a source of more local friends, as well, since you can become friends with their friends.

LINGUISTIC GOALS AND STRATEGIES
When traveling abroad for an extended period in a non-English speaking country, it is recommended that you plan to learn some of the language. While English is fairly wide-spoken in many countries, you will find that this may only be true in very large cities and may be limited to tourist areas. In considering your

cultural goals as discussed earlier, knowing the local language will also make it much easier to socialize while abroad. Of course, for many people choosing to go abroad, this is an opportunity to use their foreign language and it may be one of the primary reasons for their trip. But whether you are already fairly proficient in the language or a true beginner, there are language goals you can have for your travels.

Pre-Departure
Whether you are new to the language or you have been studying it for a long time, a good way to approach the experience is to consider what you want to be able to do with the language during your stay. This can help you decide where to focus your attention in choosing language tutorials or vocabulary to study. For example, do you want to order food and drinks? Will you want to be sure you know how to understand directions? Would you like to make small talk with native speakers? Is it your goal to have longer conversations? Do you want to make friends and participate in a variety of activities? We suggest making a small list of pre-departure goals for language tasks that you hope to do. The more specific you can make your tasks, the more defined and realistic your goals will be.

It is a good idea to plan for some language study pre-departure. This will help you feel a little less lost when you first arrive and find yourself suddenly surrounded by the language. For self-study, consider tutorial videos, language-learning podcasts, or language-learning apps. These are often designed for people to fit their language learning into their daily routine with shorter lessons. You might also choose to take a language class or work with a one-on-one tutor. Keep in mind though that language classes may have more of an academic focus rather than a travel focus and you may receive more comprehensive language lessons. If you have taken several language classes already, you should look closely at your goals and try to identify any gaps in your knowledge or any areas that might need a good refresher. For example, directions are often taught in beginning-level language courses, but they are rarely repeated at higher levels. If you are an intermediate-level student, it might be a good idea to review that navigation vocabulary because you are almost certain to need it abroad.

Since most of your interaction in the language will be face-to-face communication while you travel, we suggest focusing your time on listening and speaking skills. If you can find someone willing to practice conversational skills with you, that is ideal. As mentioned earlier, a good way to find a conversation partner is through a conversational exchange program where you trade off conversations between your target language and English. You can do this at home too before you go abroad. Several websites put people in contact with each other for multilingual conversation practice and tend to be free of charge. If you cannot find a conversation partner, you can practice conversation alone through audio or video recording. Try making a short video where you introduce yourself. Record a voice note of your to-do list for the week. Choose a topic that you love and see how long you can speak about it without any prompting. Even if you never share the recordings with anyone else, the act of making them will help you get comfortable speaking in your new language.

While Abroad

Start small and focus on your primary goals first. Interacting with people in customer service contexts (cafés, restaurants, public transportation, or shops) is a good place to try out your knowledge. These are good because the conversations are fairly routine and do not require extended discussion (in most cases). Remember though that these people usually have to wait on other customers, so you should not try to have small talk with them. As we mentioned in chapter 4, unlike in the United States, many customer service workers are not expected to make small talk with clients in other countries. (We recommend that you review the cultural practices for service encounters and small talk before departure as part of your cultural preparation.)

Another good place to start using your language is at your temporary residence. If you are staying with a host family, you will be encouraged to interact with them and we strongly recommend that you do. Most host families are used to foreigners and are patient and willing to let you try to communicate. If you are living in an apartment building or student resident hall-style building, try to start a small conversation with someone in the common areas of the building. For example, we know a student who studied in France and who was living in a student apartment building. Although her room had a kitchenette, she started cooking in the larger communal kitchen because it allowed her to say hello to her fellow residents. She ended up meeting a good friend that way, making her stay in France much more enjoyable.

Social groups are perhaps the best way to have longer and more varied conversations. If you are studying abroad, chances are you will not have as much time for conversation on campus as you do at your US school. Classes abroad may be more lecture-based and do not often have discussions or allow students to interact very much. Instead of relying on classes, participating in a social group that has regular meetings is a great way to increase your opportunities for language use. There are two ways to approach finding a social group: you can look for an activity similar to one you do back home, or you can try a new activity that may be special to the country or region. The previous examples show this. One woman we know enjoyed singing in her school choir and decided to join a choral group during her study abroad. Another woman decided to try out skiing and joined a local beginner ski group. In both cases, the two women interacted with locals in a fun and low-stakes fashion.

Fluency

In considering linguistic goals for your stay abroad, we should mention fluency as this is often a goal that we hear. While a longer stay abroad in the target language community can result in increases in your language proficiency and speaking ability, this is not a guarantee. If you are a beginner, you are likely to see larger increases in your abilities, while those of you at more intermediate and advanced levels may only see moderate to small changes. This is due to beginners having more to learn and the overall nature of language learning. In any case, many factors can lead to significant increases in your linguistic abilities during your stay abroad. The three largest seem to be the amount of time spent abroad, the quantity of interaction in the language, and the quality of that interaction. If you are abroad for six weeks, you will likely see changes in your skills, but this is dependent on what you do within those six weeks. If you spend most of your time around other English speakers, chances are you will only see mild improvement. However, if you seek out interaction with locals and try to have longer and more challenging conversations, you will increase your chances for greater improvement. We will go more in-depth about language learning during study abroad in chapter 6.

TOURISTIC GOALS AND STRATEGIES

When preparing to study abroad, it is also important to strategically plan what types of tourism you want to participate in and how you are going to go about doing it. Given the temporary nature of study abroad, you may want to have a relatively firm plan about what you want to experience at the beginning of your sojourn. Time will fly by. At the same time, be flexible to allow for spontaneity. It is also important to plan your tourism because you will need to make sure that your touristic goals align with your social, cultural, and linguistic goals. You don't want to spend all of your time outside of Germany if you have a linguistic goal of gaining fluency in German!

No matter where you go as a tourist, you should investigate the types of activities available in that region. Travel books exist for many places you are considering. If you can't find a travel book, read blogs and online forums to get ideas of what to see and what to avoid from people who were there.

Local Tourism

The most important touristic activities you may participate in could be the ones that are right outside your door because those are the activities that will help you get to know and integrate into your host community. Examples of local tourism may be visiting local landmarks and buildings, such as museums, monuments, and religious sites. Seek out opportunities to participate in local cultural practices. If you are studying abroad in Mexico in September, consider finding an Independence Day celebration in your city to celebrate along with the local people. Nature will also be a good source of touristic activities. No matter if you are in the tropics or the tundra, take walks, bike rides, and boat rides that allow you to see the natural side of your host community.

Local citizens are excellent sources for learning about what activities should be experienced to learn about life in that community. Therefore, we recommend you utilize the social connections you have made at school and in your living situation to figure out what celebrations to make sure you make it to, what museums are a must-see, and what restaurants are unavoidable. Maybe they will even go with you!

Regional and International Travel

When you are spending an extended time in a different part of the world, it is natural that you will want to experience places that you don't normally have easy access to. Admittedly, Josh spent a full Holy Week in Greece while studying abroad elsewhere in

Europe and it was one of the best parts of the whole academic year abroad. He gained a new perspective on history and civilization that he never would have obtained in his native Midwestern United States. The same can be said for traveling to other regions of the host country. When you are studying abroad in Brazil, it is expected that you may want to visit large cities, beaches, and a jungle.

The need to strategically plan regional and international travel becomes clear when you consider that any time spent in other places is time spent *away* from your host community and its people. So, if you have social, cultural, or linguistic goals that can only be achieved successfully within your host community, it will be important to not leave that community very often. Think about when you would probably travel away from your host community. It would probably be during weekends or holidays because those are times when you are not in class. Now think about when people you meet abroad would be free from work to hang out with you. That would probably also be weekends or holidays. Again, if you are consistently away, you are robbing yourself of valuable time in your host community.

This doesn't mean that you have to avoid travel. You shouldn't! However, it is important to moderate that travel. If you are abroad for a semester or an academic year, consider traveling during one weekend a month. This will mean that you still get to take numerous trips but it also will allow you to spend the majority of your weekends in your host community.

Occasionally, you may take some of your host community with you. Consider finding ways to travel with local people. For example, we know a woman who joined a church group that took regular trips to other cities and campsites. It was a way for her to still travel while not being separated from locals. If this isn't possible, it can be very rewarding to travel with other study-abroad students or alone. You may learn a great deal by traveling with international students from other countries, such as their cultural practices. They can also be great conversation partners in the second language.

Traveling Responsibly

Keep in mind, while traveling to other places during your study abroad sojourn, it is just as important to recognize linguistic and cultural differences in the place that you visit as it is in your actual host country. Be courteous to other travelers and people you encounter. Be open to new cultural practices such as food and drink, social life, and beliefs. You want people in that community to have good impressions of you and the country you represent.

Also, you will want to be financially responsible since money is a frequent impediment to study abroad activities. In many parts of the world, you can save money by staying in reputable hostels, flying on discount airlines, and buying food in markets. Of course, when making any such arrangements, read reviews or consult with travel professionals to make sure other people have felt safe and satisfied in the past. Additionally, you can obtain discounts in some places by getting the International Student Identity Card (ISIC) or something similar where you live. A search in 2022 shows that this card provides discounts for tours, entry tickets, travel, and even a cat café in Perth, Australia.

ACADEMIC GOALS AND STRATEGIES

If you are going abroad as part of an academic study program, then having clear academic goals is important. While it is highly likely that you will be enjoying a more exciting and fun social life while abroad, you need to keep in mind that your study abroad is a key part of continuing your education and is not a vacation from school. You can still enjoy your tourism and social goals while abroad, but you will want to be sure to keep them in balance with your academic goals.

Pre-Departure

Setting your academic goals begins with selecting the right program for your overall academic goals. To recap what we discussed in chapter 1, we review the following suggestions. First, meet with your academic advisors early on to discuss your plans for study abroad (if you have a major and a minor, you will want to meet with both advisors). This will help you have a good sense of when it will be best for you to go abroad and what types of courses you should plan to take while there. You should also meet with someone from your school's study abroad office to discuss your academic plan. If your university has a faculty-led program, this might be a very short and easy meeting because there are usually required courses that are predetermined for the trip. However, in many cases it will be up to you to select your courses and figure out the equivalent courses at your university. This may require finding detailed course descriptions or a sample syllabus of the course.

Second, when selecting your courses at the foreign institution, again, we recommend looking for classes that are unique and cannot be taken at your home university. One of the special aspects of study abroad is the opportunity to expand your academic horizons through these types of distinctive courses. Those classes may help you explore new areas of interest that are not always available to you at your home institution. You may discover new topics of study for you that will help guide your future career or postgraduate study. Additionally, choosing unique courses will make it easier to select classes for your following semesters back on campus because you will not have to worry about repeating material or taking courses outside your area simply to meet the credit requirements.

Third, as you look at the course offerings at the foreign university, make a couple of different course plans. Study abroad program websites may provide you with a broad description of possible courses that you can take, but just as with US universities, not all courses can be offered every semester. You can create a few plans that you like and when it is time to enroll in courses you will be prepared to be flexible if your first choices are not available.

Finally, as you plan for your courses, be certain that the courses you are selecting are sufficiently academically rigorous to be considered as transfer credits for your university. For example, many study abroad programs offer supplemental culture and community courses that are fun and interesting to students, but that might not count as transfer credits. A class on the history of wine that includes a weekly wine tasting might be fun for you to learn about the local culture, but it probably will not be considered academically sufficient for your home institution. (Of course, you can still take the fun wine class as part of your extracurricular activities to help you learn more about local culture.)

WHILE ABROAD

Being successful as a student during your study abroad is not too different from achieving success at home, in that you will still need to keep up with the material, attend class, and put forth sufficient time and effort in your assignments. However, there are some key elements to keep in mind, as you are away from home, in particular, the classroom culture, balancing study time with fun time, and recognizing differences in grading.

When you first attend your classes at your foreign institution, you will want to pay attention to the classroom culture. Your new school may have a more traditional approach where the professor lectures and students are expected to listen quietly and take notes. Other schools may encourage rich student engagement and robust class discussion. You will need to observe the local students to gain an understanding of the expectations of students and then work to meet those expectations. This will likely also mean observing how other students address the professor and whether or not it is acceptable to question the professor's viewpoints. In the United States we are often much more informal; professors may be fine with you using their first name or expressing your opposing opinion in class. However, in other countries this behavior may be seen as rude or inappropriate. You should also note that the use of technology might vary greatly from the United States where you are accustomed to using your laptop in class for note-taking. In several foreign environments, the use of a laptop during class is frowned upon.

During your study abroad, you will want to spend your free time exploring your new surroundings and making the most of being in another country. We understand that and we certainly encourage you to take the opportunity to explore the local culture. Nonetheless, you are also there to learn and you will want to make sure you are taking the time you need to study and prepare for class. If you are taking classes in your second language, this might mean additional study time, as work in your second language usually requires more time for processing readings and producing written work. Additionally, you are likely to have less structure in your schedule during study abroad because you are not doing your other school activities. For some students this freedom is almost too much, and they end up spending all their time out and about enjoying what the local community has to offer. You need to find the right balance so that you still have the time to enjoy yourself, while still remembering your duties as a student.

Finally, as a student you should be aware that grading can vary greatly from country to country. As well, your foreign classes may only base your grade on a few major assignments. For example, grades may not be given for participation or homework at foreign universities. Outside of the United States, there is also less concern with achieving the highest possible grade and professors will often reserve those high grades for only the very best students in their class. A grade equivalent to a B may be seen as a rather good grade at a foreign school. Likewise, giving out the equivalent of a C can be viewed as normal for acceptable work. This can be frustrating to American students who are used to receiving As for most assignments and are often very GPA-driven. It is important to remember that while you may not receive the highest GPA of your academic career when you study abroad, you will still have incredible learning experiences that far outweigh any grade you may receive.

How Types of Goals Intersect

Did you notice that any of your cultural and social goals may be similar or related in some way? Did you find yourself reconsidering your tourism goals after deciding what your linguistic goals may be? Many times, someone's cultural goals can be essentially social goals because they both can involve integrating into the local life of the community and learning about cultural practices. Additionally, social, linguistic, and cultural goals can also intersect with tourism goals. If you wish to be integrated into local communities and speak their languages, you should plan your tourist activities so that you are around your local community as much as possible. While it may be very tempting to travel to nearby places any time you have free time, that is also the time you will have to become a member of your local community.

We hope this chapter has helped you plan for the types of goals you want to achieve during your time abroad, as well as how you could go about accomplishing those goals. When you get to your housing abroad, take the list of goals you made while reading this chapter and post it in a place you will see easily, such as above your desk. Also, you should be open to adapting your goals if you change your mind. Similarly, if you find a strategy is not working, you should change it too.

CHAPTER 6

Language Learning and Study Abroad

IF YOU ARE ALREADY A LANGUAGE STUDENT OR HAVE AN INTER-
est in learning a foreign language, chances are you see your study
abroad as a key component in helping you achieve a higher proficiency in that language. Study abroad provides language learners
with an array of opportunities for interaction with a second language in all its real-world contexts. Additionally, most students
choose to continue with their language courses abroad, helping
them to have additional structured lessons in the classroom, as
well as having the experience of living in the target language
community. Sometimes there is a misconception that you must
reach a particular level of language proficiency before you should
study abroad. The truth is you can study abroad at any time in your
language learning career; nonetheless, you will have a different
experience at different proficiency levels.

What about people going abroad who are not language students? As mentioned in the previous chapter, we recommend that
before your stay abroad, you consider doing some language study.
This does not mean that you must enroll in a course; there are
many options for at-home self-study that are available to you for
free or at very low cost. Many of these options are designed to be
entertaining and we recommend looking for activities that you
enjoy to keep yourself interested in practicing the language. Even

if you only have time for a few weeks of study before you go, any amount of language prep will help you in a non-English-speaking country. While it may be possible that there will be English speakers in your destination country, you should not assume that they will always be available to help you navigate your way through your daily activities.

One small thing to note, in this chapter, we will use the term "second language" to describe the language you are learning and using during your time in your host country. This is a general term that refers to any language that you learn after your native language.

REALISTIC GOALS

As language professors, we often hear students tell us that they want to study abroad because they "want to be fluent" in their language. While achieving fluency may be possible for some students who go abroad, it is often not a realistic goal for many students. It is important to recognize that study abroad is not a magic key to language fluency. While the definition of fluency can vary, what most students tend to mean is they want to speak the language with minimal effort in a variety of contexts and to be generally understood by most native speakers.[1] This type of language ability usually comes when learners reach an advanced level of language proficiency, and often, this is after multiple years of classes and study abroad. If you have already been taking language courses for a few years and have reached the fifth or sixth semester of university-level language classes, you may find that study abroad can provide you with that final push toward language fluency. However, if you are newer in your language learning experience, you will likely not find yourself fluent after your study abroad program, despite still making significant improvements in your language skills.

Your language learning success while abroad is highly dependent on a variety of factors, some of which may be out of your control, but others should be part of your overall plan for your study abroad if language learning is one of your goals. The three largest factors to consider include the amount of exposure you have to the language, the quality of the interaction you have with native speakers, and the length of your stay abroad.

To learn a second language, you must have exposure to the language, or what we call "input." This input can be oral or written, and it provides you with the necessary components of the language that will help you learn.[2] This input also needs to be at a level that you can understand, or close to it, so that you can get the gist of the message.[3] If the language that you hear and see is too difficult, it will not matter that you are exposed to it all day long. Even if you are at a very advanced level, you will discover that it is impossible to understand and pay attention to all the language around you. Say for example you are riding the metro to classes or work. You might be able to hear part of someone's conversation and understand it, but chances are you will not be able to pick out all the conversations around you, read all the signs and advertisements on the train, and process all that information while trying to remember to get off at your correct stop. The important element to keep in mind is that you will have opportunities to hear and read the language daily, but you might find that certain activities will provide more useful language exposure than others. Melanie found that when she was riding the metro each day in Rome, she could pick up one of the free newspapers available at the station and read it on her way to and from school. This gave her about forty minutes of reading time in Italian each day.

Often students assume that because they are living in a foreign community, they will automatically be immersed in the language. While this may be the case while you are out in public, you will find that there is a lot of English in the world. In some places, even when you attempt to interact in the language, people may still respond to you in English. Additionally, you must be aware of how much you may continue to use English or your home language regularly. If we go back to the metro example, suppose you are wearing headphones and listening to your favorite podcast in your home language while riding the train. This means that you automatically will not hear any of the languages around you, and while you could still see signs, your brain will likely not be able to divide the time between your home language and your other language. As wonderful as our technology is, it has created a complication for study abroad since it provides ample content in your native language that you are generally accustomed to accessing multiple times a day.[4] However, for every minute that you spend reading, watching, or listening to that content, that is every minute you are not processing and using the second language in which you want to be immersed. Likewise, you are probably used to communicating with friends and family regularly using technology, and it is natural that while you are abroad you will want to keep in touch with them. However, as you continue texting, calling, or video chatting with people back home which will increase your daily home language usage, you are again taking yourself out of an immersive second language environment.

As part of your pre-departure language preparation, we suggest considering ways to incorporate more of your second language into your daily routine through your technology use. This will be a way to increase your regular exposure to the language and you can tie it to activities you already enjoy in your first language. For example, in your second language, you could look for a playlist of popular songs, follow social media accounts from your destination country, listen to a podcast, or watch videos. To take these a step further, you could work to create your own content in the language. The idea is to choose something that you would normally do, but simply try it in your second language. If you get used to doing these activities at home first, you will provide yourself with additional language learning in a fun way, but also you will be able to continue doing these activities while you are abroad.

In addition to increasing your language exposure before you go, we also suggest that you talk to your friends and family about cutting back on communication while abroad. Naturally you will still want to keep in touch with them and let them know that you are staying safe and healthy, but if you can decrease your texting and calls, it will help in two key ways. First, it will help you stay more immersed in your second language environment because you will simply be interacting less in your home language. The more time you spend texting and talking in your home language the more it will take you away from doing activities in the community. Also, although you will become more acclimated to switching between languages, this can be very tiring at first, and the temptation to only use your home language will be strong. Second, you will feel less homesick if you spend less time talking to people back home. This one may seem unusual, but we find that the more someone is focused on what is happening at home, the more they feel that they are missing out or wishing they were with those friends and family.

While the amount of exposure to the language is important, you should also think about the quality of the interactions that you can have in the language. Suppose you go to the same café every morning for breakfast when you are abroad. Each day you greet the server and order your food and drink, having a nice little conversation in your second language. Quantity-wise you could count that as a daily morning conversation with a native speaker but consider the quality of your interaction. While you may change up your order from day to day, you are likely to use rather basic language with basic structures, and your conversation is very limited to food and drink vocabulary. Once you have mastered this conversation, probably after a couple of orders, you will not be making any progress in your second language. To gain more from conversations with a native speaker, you need to have conversations that use a variety of topics that do not follow a set pattern and allow you to be creative with the language.[5] Even as a beginner, you will want to remember to challenge yourself to have different conversations with native speakers, when possible, that will allow you to try out a variety of skills, and that will provide you with more diverse language. While the quantity of your language input is certainly important, we know that learners who see greater changes in their language are those who have also had greater quality of interaction.[6]

To increase the quality of your interactions, you will need to think about when and where you will spend time with native speakers while abroad. Usually, higher-quality interactions are possible when you get to know someone better as an acquaintance or a friend. This should be a consideration in your pre-departure planning. For example, if you have the option of living with a host family or living with other foreign students, selecting the host family provides a greater likelihood of developing a relationship with the family and having higher-quality conversations. While living with other foreign students, you will quickly discover that most of them speak English or that their language skills are limited like yours. Speaking to someone at your same language level might provide you with some practice, but it won't challenge you and allow for more language development as would a conversation with a native speaker. Your living situation will not be your only possible connection to native speakers, however, so you should think about other contexts where you can increase your chances of meeting native speakers and fostering relationships.

Your ability to interact with native speakers and develop friendships is also often highly dependent on the length of your stay in the foreign community. If you are going for a shorter period, say a four-week program, you might not have as much time for interacting with native speakers. Building a friendship in your first language takes time, and as you can imagine, it is often a slower process in your second language. This is not to say that you can't make friends with someone during a shorter stay, but simply to demonstrate that it is more likely to happen if you can travel for longer. Also, you should be aware that native speakers may be less interested in making friends with someone who is only around for a short period. When Melanie interviewed US students studying abroad in Costa Rica, a popular study destination, several of the interviewees lamented that the local students weren't interested in hanging out or becoming friends because they knew the US students were leaving soon.[7] Likewise, you may be limited in the types of extracurricular activities that you are available to participate in based on the length of your stay. If you are only in the country for a few weeks, you might not want to dedicate a large block of time to a weekly event. If you are abroad longer, you may participate in more extracurricular activities with local people which could lead to more language learning.[8]

As we suggested in chapter 5, as part of your pre-departure language preparation, we recommend finding ways to interact with native speakers of your second language before you go abroad. This may take some creativity and use of online resources if there are few native speakers of your language in your home community. If you are at college or live near a college campus, you might check for language tables (usually a weekly meeting where people converse in the language) or international events as a way to connect with native speakers. Online, you can look for people who speak your language on social media or find a tandem language partner to practice communication skills. Even if you only have minimal contact with a native speaker before you go abroad, you will feel less intimidated when you arrive at your destination country.

As mentioned earlier, the length of your stay can also influence which language skills you can improve. Some skills, like general speaking ability, can show marked improvement in the shorter term.[9] However, other skills, like understanding the nuances of polite conversation, usually require a longer period to observe and experience how native speakers achieve that.[10] When you are considering how long to travel, you should think about your specific language goals and consider what you hope to do at the end of your study abroad experience. In general, short-term stays of six weeks or fewer usually result in greater changes for people starting as beginners or at an early intermediate level. For more advanced students, the changes are more subtle. Comparing this to a full semester abroad of approximately thirteen to sixteen weeks, learners at all levels are often able to improve by at least one proficiency level, however, improvements in different skill areas vary greatly.[11] Though, for more advanced learners the changes are not as drastic. Finally, for longer-term programs for a full academic year of twenty-six weeks or more, the greatest changes are seen at all levels. Again though, you should keep in mind that there are more factors involved than just how long you are abroad.

RESEARCHING THE LANGUAGE OF THE HOST COMMUNITY

While you are planning your trip, you want to be sure to include research on the languages and the language varieties that are spoken in that country, particularly in the region where you plan to live. While you may know that your second language is widely spoken there, it is important to recognize that certain regions may not speak that language as intensely or that the variety of the language could be quite different from the one you have studied. For example, in China the regional dialects are so different they can be classified as separate languages. Therefore, if you want to study Mandarin Chinese you might want to reconsider a program in Hong Kong where Cantonese is more commonly spoken.[12]

If you are already studying a language that is spoken in multiple countries, you are probably already aware that regional varieties or dialects exist in that language. However, even languages that are only spoken in one country will have dialects, and it is helpful to know something about those dialects before you arrive. For some languages, you may find a lot of information written about the dialect, particularly if you are going to a popular study abroad or tourist destination. For others, it may take more searching if your language is less widely studied. If you are already in a language class, we recommend asking your instructor for information about the dialect or for ideas on obtaining information about that dialect. If you are not in a language course, we suggest finding language samples online by looking for media that comes from that region. Television shows, movies, and social media posts can be good sources to show you how people speak with everyday language.

In addition to regional varieties, there are also social differences that should be recognized before you go abroad. These can be rather complex and, in some cases, affect politeness, so knowing a little bit before you travel can help you avoid awkward situations. Again, looking for materials on polite speech, polite and impolite gestures, and general social interaction can be valuable. In most societies, there is a difference in language variety based on generation. While you may spend most of your time at school with people your age, you will likely be interacting with older people as well either as your professors, your coworkers, your boss, or your homestay family. We strongly suggest finding information about speaking to people who are older than you so that you can be sure to demonstrate politeness, especially in your first meeting. For instance, in many East Asian languages, there are special titles that are used with people based on their relationship to you. In Japanese, for example, the title *senpai* is used with older people while *sensei* is used for your instructors. Even if you do not know all the intricacies of the honorific system, using the proper title can show that you are attempting to be polite and respectful.

In considering language varieties, many students tend to think only about accents as they are often the most noticeable differences between the variety they are used to and the one in their destination country. However, language variation also includes differences in vocabulary, sentence structure, word structure, and social language use. While locals may understand the variety of language that you use, you may experience difficulty understanding their variety. Well-documented variations are easy to study and prepare for use. For example, if you study Spanish, you are probably familiar with the *you* forms of *tú*, *usted*, and *ustedes*, and you may have also been introduced to the *vosotros* form, the second person informal plural used exclusively in Spain. This form has its own verb conjugations that are usually printed in all Spanish textbooks in the United States. Nonetheless, there is a fifth form of *you* that is not widely studied in the United States, the *vos* form. This is a second person informal singular form that is commonly used in Central and South America, and yet it is rare to find *vos* and its conjugations in a textbook. It is important to remember that some less commonly familiar varieties may not be possible to study before you depart.

Studying abroad is one of the best ways to understand a dialect and language variation, particularly as some elements are better experienced than researched. Sometimes just being aware that this type of variation exists is helpful to allow you to be prepared to hear and see it.

STUDYING ABROAD AT DIFFERENT PROFICIENCY LEVELS

As stated previously, you can go abroad with any level of language ability and still have a successful experience. That being said, it helps to have an understanding of where you should focus your efforts based on your language level before you go.

BEGINNING LEVEL

If you are a true beginner with limited or no language experience, we recommend you focus your efforts on basic speaking and listening skills. Think about the encounters you are likely to have with native speakers and focus on learning vocabulary and phrases related to those encounters. To help you start thinking about what vocabulary you should learn, we have provided the following list of topics:

- basic greetings
- how to introduce yourself
- how to ask if the other person speaks your home language
- numbers—important for understanding prices, times, and distance
- food and drink
- basic descriptive adjectives—words like small, big, much, few
- basic directions and basic location prepositions—be sure to know words like right, left, turn, go straight, here, and there
- public transportation
- yes/no questions
- how to say you need help

If you are doing any type of guided lessons, either with a class or with some other type of learning program, you will likely be introduced to more vocabulary and some basic grammar. While grammar is important for becoming more advanced in the language, at the very beginning level, your primary focus should be on being intelligible rather than on being grammatically accurate every time. For example, if you're in Italy and you're hungry, if you can say *Io fame* (I hungry) it will still get your point across just as well as the grammatically correct sentence *Io ho fame* (I am hungry). Likewise, if you are learning a language with a different writing system, many beginning-level courses will spend a lot of time learning the characters or new alphabet system. However, needing to read and write will not be an immediate concern for you when you go abroad beyond understanding the very basics, like reading street signs.

If you are a little more advanced, but still in the beginning level, you will want to pay more attention to basic grammar, particularly how simple sentences are formed and how verbs work in the present tense. This will make it easier for people to understand you and will also often make them more interested in speaking with you. You should also consider expanding your vocabulary knowledge to talk about basic everyday subjects that will help you get to know people better. Some areas to consider studying include:

- hobbies and sports
- family
- descriptive adjectives
- informative questions—so you can keep the other person speaking
- school—if you are a student
- work—if you will be working abroad
- health or sickness—useful if you need to explain to someone that you are sick

At the beginning level you can expect to see a great many changes in your language abilities while you are abroad, even if you are participating in a short-term program. Most beginners will see the greatest changes in their speaking abilities and their confidence while speaking.[13] You will probably also show good improvement in your listening abilities as this goes along with conversational interaction. Your vocabulary will expand quite a lot based on the activities you do the most, and you are likely to have a better sense of grammar, although you may not see drastic changes in your abilities to produce grammatically correct sentences. Most likely, by the end of your study abroad experience, you will be able to carry on short conversations about everyday topics with most people.

INTERMEDIATE LEVEL

If you are at the intermediate level, you probably already know basic conversations and have made progress in the four main areas of speaking, listening, reading, and writing. Like the beginners, we recommend you spend your pre-departure preparation focused on speaking and listening as these tend to still be students' weakest areas or areas where people often lack confidence. Nonetheless, we suggest working on more complex conversation skills that will allow you to talk more in-depth about a topic. These are often thought of as conversation strategies and include elements such as:

- asking follow-up questions to obtain more information and keep your partner speaking
- providing your opinion and the reasons behind your ideas
- giving more detailed descriptions
- using circumlocution to describe a thing or concept when you lack the proper word
- asking for language advice or explanations
- finding ways to explain that you don't understand but are trying to
- successfully ending a conversation

In addition to focusing on those topics, it is beneficial to review some of the vocabulary from your early studies. These are words that you likely learned early on but might not have used in frequent speech or in class. A brief list to help you focus is:

- numbers
- directions and location terms
- food and drink
- public transportation

• health or sickness

At this point in your learning, you have probably studied more about grammar and are likely to know how to create more complex sentences. While it is always recommended to try to use the grammar that you know, once again just know that you don't need to be perfect to carry on a conversation. Often native speakers are willing to overlook grammar errors if you are still intelligible.[14] The important thing to remember is that even if you messed up the tense or used the wrong gender for a noun, the other person is likely to still understand your general meaning. You will even get better at recovering when you aren't understood. When Josh mixed up the words for scissors and fabric, his listener had no idea what he was saying. He realized he could use actions to be understood. Then, they both laughed about the situation. From a language learning perspective, just trying to interact with native speakers regularly is key to making the most of your time abroad. Remember too that most people are not concerned about judging your speech and will usually be happy that you are trying to speak their language.

Intermediate students will usually show a great deal of improvement in their language skills, often moving up to the advanced proficiency level after study abroad. Intermediate learners tend to improve most in interpersonal skills, particularly in their ability to have longer conversations,[15] their knowledge of social cues and politeness,[16] an increase in their vocabulary,[17] and an increase in their understanding of regional varieties.[18] Intermediate students also tend to show an increase in their self-confidence in their language abilities and a decrease in anxiety when it comes to using their language. Yet, typically there is little change seen in grammatical abilities overall.

ADVANCED LEVEL

If you have been studying the language for a long time, chances are you already feel fairly comfortable with your abilities and interacting with the language in general. For your pre-departure preparation, we suggest focusing on the skills in which you feel least confident and looking for new methods to practice those skills, preferably with media created for native speakers. For example, if you want to work on your listening skills, try finding a podcast or television show (watch without subtitles) that comes from your destination country. At this level, you are also more inclined to start noticing the subtle differences in social language use that less advanced students are not yet capable of recognizing. Consider language tasks that we do regularly, such as:

- greeting people
- thanking someone
- making a request
- complimenting someone
- refusing an invitation
- inviting someone to do something
- making plans
- apologizing
- talking about past events

Look for examples of these types of everyday speech tasks in native speaker media to see how they are done. Sometimes you might see that the formulaic way that you were taught to do something from your classes and textbooks is not exactly the way that real people speak. Again, media that comes from your destination country is ideal because these types of tasks can vary greatly between communities. It will also be beneficial to simply heighten your awareness of this type of speech because you will be more likely to pay attention to it when you arrive.

As with the intermediate level, we recommend reviewing some of the basic vocabulary related to travel and everyday life that you might not have thought much about since your first language classes:

- numbers
- directions and location prepositions
- food and drink
- public transportation
- health or sickness

Seeing as you are already quite proficient in your language, you should not anticipate seeing drastic changes in your abilities. However, this is not to say that you will not make improvements; you simply have fewer improvements to make at your level. We tend to see the greatest changes with advanced students who spend more time interacting with native speakers. Since your ability to communicate is much greater than lower-level students, you will have greater opportunities to make friends and get involved with the local community. We highly encourage you to do this if making language gains is a primary goal for you. (As we mention in other chapters, getting involved with locals provides other wonderful elements too.) Advanced students tend to see changes in speaking skills, social language skills, vocabulary, and their knowledge of regional variety.[19] Many advanced students also find a rise in their self-confidence and a reduction in language use anxiety. While some advanced students find that they improve in their grammar, this is not always the case, and in general, study abroad does not seem to have a great influence on improving grammatical accuracy, particularly during speaking.

Final Thoughts about Language Learning

Whether you have a lot of time to dedicate to your pre-departure language study or only a few weeks, whatever you do to prepare will be useful when you arrive in your destination country. We hope that by understanding a little more about the language learning process and by focusing your attention as we suggest, you will get more out of this preparation than if you went in blind. Remember to try to do fun activities in the language that will help you enjoy learning. A lot of students use flashcards to study vocabulary, but they often find them boring and stop using them quickly. Instead, if you try doing word games to practice your vocabulary, you will likely find the challenge of the game more entertaining and be more likely to keep practicing. Remember too that any amount of practice is useful, and will pay off for you when you arrive.

The key to being successful at language learning, especially while abroad, is to keep trying. There will be times when you try to communicate and it will fail (this happens at all levels). However, the best thing you can do is to remind yourself that it's OK to fail and to keep trying because next time you could be successful, and it could lead to something great. There will certainly be times when using the language feels weird or awkward, but as you work to push through those uncomfortable times, you will find that the more you use your second language the more natural it will become.

CHAPTER 7

Study Abroad Outside of College

LIFE AS AN UNDERGRADUATE STUDENT IS A BUSY TIME WHEN people are juggling obligations related to academics, work, activities, families, and beyond. For many people, this may make study abroad seem impossible, even if they have a strong desire to go. Other people may be hoping to have additional international experiences before starting a full-time job. Because of this, it is important to remember that experiences similar to undergraduate study abroad can still happen after the completion of that degree. In this chapter, we discuss popular opportunities for you to participate in postgraduate international programs that include graduate study and/or research, assisting in teaching English, service, and more. Before detailing many types of experiences, we present information about one of the most prominent opportunities open to US citizens: Fulbright's US Student Program.

FULBRIGHT US STUDENT PROGRAM

The Fulbright Program is a federally sponsored program, which was created by the US Congress in the 1940s and named for Senator J. William Fulbright of Arkansas, that seeks to "foster mutual understanding between nations, advance knowledge across communities, and improve lives around the world."[1] While many Fulbright awards are awarded to university faculty and administrators, in this chapter we focus on awards for which students who recently finished their undergraduate degrees are eligible, the English Teaching Assistantships and Study/Research Awards, which make up the Student Program.

The US Student Program grants are open to any US citizen who has completed an undergraduate degree by the time their award period begins. While in the country, Fulbright recipients receive a stipend that is meant to help with living expenses, health coverage, round-trip airfare, and other benefits that may be offered in some locations, such as tuition, research funds, or dependent support. Interested applicants should check out us.fulbrightonline.org to browse countries and awards.

Do note that the application is lengthy and should be started months in advance of the typical October deadline. For both types of grants, applicants complete a series of tasks that include demographic and personal history information, a personal statement, a statement of grant purpose, and some short answer questions, among other items. You also will provide a transcript of all postsecondary work (unofficial transcripts suffice at the time of application) and will participate in an interview on your home campus. You do not have to do this alone. Current students and alumni have access to their home university's Fulbright Program Advisor, a faculty or staff member who helps guide applicants through the process. It is never too early or too late to contact your university's Fulbright Program Advisor. Even first-year undergraduate students can benefit from getting early information! After the national deadline, typically in October, applications are reviewed by committees in the United States and in the host country. Some host countries choose to interview select candidates.

STUDY AND RESEARCH GRANTS AND FELLOWSHIPS
What Are These Awards?

The first type of international experience we will discuss in this chapter involves the recipient's academic progress. Even though most students who study abroad are undergraduates, it is quite possible to take graduate classes and research abroad after completing your undergraduate degree. In this section, we take a look at some of the possible ways you could do this.

OPEN STUDY AND RESEARCH WITH THE FULBRIGHT US STUDENT PROGRAM

Studying abroad as a graduate student or completing a research project can be a costly experience. One way for qualified US citizens to conduct such work is by applying for an Open Study and Research grant through the Fulbright US Student Program. In 2022, the program's website reported awards in approximately 140 countries.[2] There are two main types of grants that Fulbright funds within this category. First, applicants can apply for a grant to attend graduate school abroad with Fulbright funding. Typically, the applicant needs to apply for the chosen graduate program in addition to the Fulbright grant itself. In some countries, such as New Zealand, applicants may select any university to apply to. Meanwhile, in other countries, such as Finland, there are awards granted to attend specific universities. The duration of the awards depends on several factors including what is offered by the host university, the host country, and the recipient's academic progress and performance in the program. In some cases, the recipient may complete a one- or two-year master's program. In other cases, the recipient may take courses without pursuing a degree.

The second type of academic award funded by the Fulbright US Student Program is the research award. When applying for this type of award, applicants choose a country where research awards are offered and in which it makes sense that they conduct research and have secured the support of an individual or institution that has agreed to be the affiliate. In the application, which includes a letter from the affiliate, the applicant details their plans for the research project to be conducted abroad. During the duration of the grant, award recipients are expected to carry out the proposed project.

As an extension of the Open Study and Research awards offered by Fulbright, there are a smaller number of field-specific awards. Opportunities in the performing and fine arts awards are available for those pursuing graduate work in music, art, design, and theater, as well as for those wishing to complete projects in museums. Additionally, there are awards specifically for students and researchers in STEM fields and a limited few in journalism and business.

DEGREE PROGRAMS

A Fulbright award is not the only pathway to study abroad as a graduate student. People interested in this type of experience can research countries and institutions on their own and apply directly to the university, just as they would in their own country. Applicants need to find programs they qualify for that would help them fulfill their academic, professional, and personal goals, just as they would when researching domestic programs. However, they also need to look into other logistical information, such as visa requirements, work requirements, and health insurance. There is also the added question of teaching methods, foreign accreditation, and language of instruction. In some countries, American students may find their classes to be more lecture-based than they experienced in their undergraduate institutions. People should also research the foreign university's accreditation, particularly if their graduate degrees are essential to the next step in the United States, such as professional licenses or doctoral programs. Finally, applicants must be cognizant to only apply for programs that are taught in languages they have at least native-like proficiency.

There are ways to complete graduate courses abroad through American institutions. Many domestic universities offer graduate study abroad, although these opportunities will be fewer than for undergraduate programs. For example, Josh, who completed his master's degree at Bowling Green State University (BGSU), spent the first year of that program at the University of Alcalá de Henares in Spain through BGSU's affiliation. Going this route provides additional support with visas, housing, academic credits, host country class expectations, and more. Interested graduate students should contact the relevant office at their graduate institution to learn more about their options.

INFORMAL STUDY

You don't need to enroll in a university to study in another country. There are opportunities for people of all ages to take courses abroad, especially if they are language courses. Around the world, there are language schools where you can take level-appropriate classes in the target language, enjoy cultural excursions, and even stay with a host family. One particular example is the Costa Rica Learning Academy in San José, Costa Rica. They offer Spanish language instruction at all levels, from beginners to advanced. They will tailor the number of sessions, the content of instruction, and activities to the individual's needs. Many such schools are reputable but they typically do not offer academic credit that can be transferred to a US university.

ENGLISH TEACHING ASSISTANT GRANTS AND FELLOWSHIPS
What Are These Awards?

Another common reason people go abroad is to work as an English teaching assistant. Typically, a recipient of such an award works part time in an English language classroom in a country where the majority language is not English. In most cases, there is a classroom teacher in the room as well. The age range depends on the award selected. In this section, we highlight a few common awards, recognizing that there are more available in the world, and highlight some personal experiences we have encountered in our careers.

AWARDS

Similar to their offerings for open study and research, the US Fulbright Student Program also offers funding and placements for US citizens to be English Teaching Assistants at all levels of education from kindergarten to university classes around the world. Recipients of an English Teaching Assistantship (ETA) serve part time as a linguistic and cultural model in a classroom while also working on an additional community engagement project meant to help fulfill the Fulbright mission of fostering mutual understanding between people of different cultures. Those who wish to apply choose a country based on the profiles the host countries prepare. In these profiles, there is information about school placements (age, urban or rural locations, etc.), language requirements, special requirements, and any other information they feel applicants need.[3]

We spoke with Hannah Dull, an ETA to Brazil directly after finishing her undergraduate degree, about her experiences working with English language students in that country. Hannah spent her time working in university-level English classes, facilitating a conversation club that was attended by students and community members, and co-creating monthly English classes for English teachers, among other activities. While working on each of these elements of her grant, she greatly enjoyed being a source as a native speaker of American English, a source of cultural knowledge, and an ambassador of the United States, particularly when she gave presentations on aspects of US life (e.g., feminism in the United States).

Before and during her stay in Brazil, Hannah felt she was well supported by Fulbright and the administration at her placement. Before starting her placement, she participated in an orientation with other ETAs in Brazil, was matched with an experienced ETA who served as her mentor, and was assisted by her local coordinator in finding housing. Throughout the year, she was visited by her mentor and she attended a midyear conference with her orientation group. Importantly, she felt supported by Fulbright in her endeavors to learn about Brazil. She got ample time away from the school which she could use to travel. Finally, keeping in mind that the stipends that Fulbright offers differ according to the situation, Hannah found her stipend was adequate to live and travel.

We asked Hannah what advice she had for readers of this chapter who are interested in being an English teaching assistant abroad. First, she recommended applying even if you don't feel you qualify for the grant. If you meet the minimum requirements, you qualify. A successful ETA does not need to have official teaching credentials in most cases. Second, an ETA recipient needs to be flexible. Not all ETAs know their placement and the exact type of work they will do even when they are flying to their host country. Hannah witnessed this with other people and she saw it worked out in each case. Finally, she urges recipients to explore and travel around their host country. Recall that Fulbright and other organizations want mutual understanding across cultures. This means you need to get out and see the country, not just work and go to your apartment.

While a Fulbright ETA is a great way to gain teaching experience abroad, it is not the only way. Many individual countries offer opportunities for native English speakers to work in English classes in their countries. The Japan Exchange and Teaching (JET) Program is a very reputable program that invites US and Canadian citizens with bachelor's degrees who hold a serious personal interest in Japan to apply to be teaching assistants in English classrooms in that country.[4] Programs in other countries feature similar placements and requirements. The English Program in Korea (EPIK) in South Korea, the Teaching Assistant Program in France (TAPIF) in France, and the North American Language and Cultural Assistants Program (NALCAP) in Spain are just a few examples.

Jennie Martell Szumski participated in the program in Spain, teaching English for two years in Seville and one year in Valencia. The process of applying is fairly easy, the application opens in late January and you need to provide proof that you've completed at least two years of university study, a passport from an English-speaking country, a letter of recommendation from a college professor, and a letter of intent. Jennie recommends getting your application completed as soon as possible because the program has become very popular and assignments are made on a first come, first serve basis. Apply early if you want to have any preference of community or city. If selected, in April you will be assigned a region and may be able to request a particular city. By May, you should know your school assignment. Work begins on October 1 and you will need to make all arrangements for travel and housing on your own. She mentioned that you will be assigned a school mentor who might potentially help you with housing arrangements or other setup arrangements, but that you should not expect to receive help from the program. She did mention that there is a WhatsApp group of program participants and a Facebook group called "Teaching in Spain" that can put you in touch with other foreign teachers who can provide advice and help for getting yourself set up in Spain.

Jennie had previously studied abroad in Spain as an under-graduate student and was an advanced Spanish speaker when she participated in this program. She found it fairly easy to find an apartment to rent and while the overall time and effort it took to get herself set up in the country wasn't easy, it wasn't overly difficult either. However, her ability to interact with native speakers was likely helpful to her in preparing to live in Spain. She did point out though that she had friends in the program who did not speak Spanish and were successful too. Most of those friends also learned Spanish during their time abroad.

In Seville, Jennie worked twelve hours a week for an $800 monthly stipend in a high school where she was always paired with a teacher. Sometimes Jennie taught in an English class where she was responsible for preparing and teaching the lessons. Other times, she taught in other content classes like biology, mathematics, or history, where the main teacher prepared the lesson and she was responsible for teaching it in English. In those cases, the main teacher was always available for assistance if she wasn't as familiar with the topics. In Valencia, Jennie taught for sixteen hours a week for a $1,000 monthly stipend at an elementary school with students ages three to twelve. Again, she taught a variety of subjects, including several physical education classes with the younger children where she could give them many basic movement commands in English. She did mention that teaching in Valencia was more challenging both due to the age of the students and the fact that their first language was Valencian, which she does not speak. This was also a more challenging aspect of working with the teachers in Valencia as during breaks she couldn't interact with them as a group because they spoke Valencian whereas in Seville, she could speak to the teachers easily.

Jennie thought one of the benefits of this program is the lifestyle that it provides because the stipend is enough to enjoy Spain and its lower cost of living without dipping into your savings and you have a great deal of free time for activities while there. She made local Spanish friends, particularly through language exchange programs at language schools, which made it possible to meet people who were particularly interested in making friends with foreigners. She also spent a lot of time with other program participants because they had the same amount of free time. Jennie did mention though that at first it might seem like too much free time and some people might struggle with what to do with all that time.

In considering the challenges of the program, Jennie mentioned that dealing with the Spanish government's bureaucracy is often a nightmare, especially when extending your visa to stay longer in the country. She said she felt like she was always having to renew her visa or complete paperwork related to the visa. She also mentioned that this bureaucracy affected getting paid in Valencia and that she and the other program participants had to protest about not being paid on time. She has since heard that this is an ongoing problem in that region and that it can also happen in other regions. (She did not have this problem in Seville.) Overall though, she found the experience to be a positive one.

It is possible to apply for teaching jobs abroad on your own, as well. Kaleigh Newton did just that when she applied to teach English at a private university in Barranquilla, Colombia. She found her job through the Teachers of English to Speakers of Other Languages (TESOL) job marketplace; a well-known resource for finding international English teaching jobs. She also mentioned that she attended their yearly conference and interviewed in person at the conference as part of the career services offered by the organization.

When considering advice based on her experiences, the main element that Kaleigh wanted to share was the importance of understanding cultural differences and expectations, especially when coming from the low-context culture of the United States and going to work in a high-context culture. In low-context cultures, communication is viewed as informative, straightforward, and explicit. In high-context cultures, communication is based more on personal relationships, emotions, tone, body language, and the overall context of the communication.[5] Kaleigh mentioned that this difference was evident in elements like expecting to find centralized information as we do here in the United States versus the expectation that she should simply ask different people at work for the information. This was also present in communication with her coworkers and students. In many instances, there was an expectation for personal, face-to-face communication rather than consulting a standard document or sending an email. She also mentioned the importance of understanding the differences between "cold" cultures and "warm" cultures, indicating that if you are in a warm culture environment, this means emphasizing personal relationships and personal experiences more than quickly getting information.

Kaleigh highly recommended researching the area and city where you will be living to get a sense of the lifestyle and to find out how closely it aligns with your own. One thing she struggled with was the slower pace of life in Barranquilla and how time was viewed there. She advised finding ex-pat groups online for advice and insight into their struggles and complaints about a region. She did note that part of understanding their advice is being aware that cultural norms aren't good or bad, they are simply different. Reminding herself that something "isn't rude, it's just different" was a common occurrence, as well as being aware that there are stereotypes on both sides. Stereotypes, even ones that aren't necessarily negative, can lead to challenges. If you are planning to live in a region where foreigners aren't common, you might draw attention simply by being more exotic to the people there. Kaleigh also pointed out that it helps to know if your workplace frequently employs foreigners because this will influence how well they are at supporting you as a foreigner.

In considering overall why someone would want to teach English abroad, Kaleigh mentioned three main factors. First, she spoke about how it helped her understand foreigners in the United States with greater empathy. She explained that it's clear to comprehend why a group of people from the same cultural background might choose to live in the same area or spend time together because there is a need to spend time with people who understand you and your shared experience. Second, Kaleigh mentioned that living abroad in a non-English-speaking country is a great way to improve your language skills and that she valued the opportunity to improve her Spanish. Finally, again concerning cultural understanding, Kaleigh explained that having worked abroad has helped her to become a more patient person and better acknowledge and accept other people's differences.

Reagan Dewell had a similar experience when he taught at a private English school, specializing in extracurricular English classes, in Ube, Japan for one year. He was initially interested in the JET program, but when he was planning to teach in Japan, he realized that he should have started his JET application about two years prior. He did however find his job easily and said that there were many opportunities for teaching English in Japan. He found his job through Dave's ESL Café (www.eslcafe.com) a well-known site for people looking to teach English abroad.

Reagan pointed out that finding a job in Japan as a white, blond American did make the process easier, as in his experience, Japanese English schools prefer to hire exotic-looking foreigners who appear as native English speakers to them. In some ways though this can mean that they downplay teaching credentials, which can lead to some questionable teachers who are not well prepared to teach English. As someone who had training and had earned a TESL/TEFL teaching certificate before his teaching experience, Reagan felt better prepared than some of the other English teachers he encountered in Japan. Reagan also pointed out that initially he had wanted to teach English in Germany, where he had previously studied abroad. However, he found that finding an English Foreign Language (EFL) job in Japan or parts of Southeast Asia was much easier than finding a job in Germany. In his experience, Germans are not as concerned with finding native-looking or native-speaker teachers, something that he felt might be true in other areas, particularly in Northern Europe.

At his school, Reagan taught all levels of English and worked with students as young as four years old in English classes, alongside their parents, all the way to adult students in their eighties. His classes were generally arranged by age group and proficiency level. The school provided him with an established curriculum and was focused on conversational English. Most of the vocabulary and main activities had already been planned out or designed by the school's owner and it was his job to facilitate those activities.

Reagan also tutored students one-on-one in private lessons and would sometimes be hired out to teach professional English to local businesses wanting to provide lessons for their employees.

Reagan explained that the school provided him with assistance for living in Japan such as helping him find housing while he was there. This type of service can be highly beneficial as while the Japanese may be very welcoming to foreigners in general, they are not always as welcoming to renting apartments to someone who may only be in the country for a short time. Also in these cases, without the help of a Japanese friend or colleague, foreigners may be charged more for housing or may not be familiar with typical Japanese customs in securing housing. One example Reagan mentioned was the idea of "key money" where a person will gift two months' rent to the landlord as a thank-you for letting the person rent the apartment. Having the help of your employer can greatly assist you in getting established in the country, and possibly help you avoid extra expenses like key money.

With the idea of cultural differences, Reagan pointed out that one important element to keep in mind is culture shock and dealing with it as a foreigner in a place where you are obviously foreign. You have to learn how to be comfortable with sticking out all the time and getting extra attention for being foreign. This could mean everything from strangers wanting to take pictures with you to people who may see you as an easy target for trouble. This doesn't mean that you should always expect problems when you are out in public, but more that you need to have that awareness of being different and standing out in the crowd. He also stated that in some ways he would receive special treatment and respect that felt not entirely deserved simply because of the way he looks. This was not expected and while it can seem nice at first, it can also be difficult to experience.

One other aspect of obviously being American in Japan meant that people only ever wanted to speak English to Reagan while he was there. He had very little opportunity to learn Japanese and did not receive any encouragement or support to learn Japanese. Before going, he did not study Japanese and after a year of being in the country, he reports that he still doesn't know any Japanese. This was largely due to his employer saying that he didn't need to worry about learning the language and their desire for him to maintain his "Americanness." In their eyes, he was there to speak English with Japanese people, not worry about spending his time learning Japanese. Reagan said that while he was certainly able to live in Japan without knowing the language, he did think it would have made things easier overall if he had at least some knowledge of the language.

Overall, Reagan felt very positive about his experience teaching English in Japan and said that it was a "once-in-a-lifetime experience" that gave him great experiences that he could never have at home. He was grateful to have had the opportunity to be fully immersed in a new culture and one that he had little experience with before going to Japan. He expressed the importance of being open to new cultural experiences and paying attention to Japanese social cues and norms to help you adjust better to living in the community. Reagan mentioned that people who are better at accepting cultural differences are those who tend to be happier and more successful while abroad.

One final thought that Reagan wanted to share is that if you are interested in teaching English abroad, you can absolutely make it happen. In his view the only thing that is standing in your way is yourself and your nerves or fears about going. He highly encourages you to do it because the experience is more worthwhile than you know.

INTERNSHIPS

Another programmatic option that would allow you to go abroad after completing your undergraduate degree is through an internship. Much like an internship during your undergraduate career (also possible abroad), an internship at this stage in your life also provides you with important professional experience in your chosen field while also giving you the chance to live and work abroad. When deciding where to go and what type of program to apply for, you should consider the type of work you would be doing, language requirements, cross-cultural similarities and differences related to work, and, importantly, labor laws regarding noncitizen interns. Common providers of such internships include the Institute of International Education of Students (IES), International Studies Abroad (ISA), and The Education Abroad Network (TEAN). Additionally, GoOverseas.com provides even more recommendations, as well as a bank of internship programs, along with user reviews. Check out websites like this one as a part of your research.

SERVICE
Volunteerism
It is not uncommon to find opportunities to volunteer in some way in another country. This type of service may involve your chosen field, your religious institution, or another passion. One example was Josh's trip to Nicaragua. This trip was organized and run by a Christian-oriented charitable group but individual travelers were responsible for paying for their own trip. Supplies were purchased through donations. The group included about twenty Americans who traveled to a remote village in Nicaragua and worked with local community members to begin construction on eight houses for vetted families. Another group helped the community complete the houses during a later trip. Josh found this to be a very effective way to learn from members of a different community, practice language skills, and work alongside Nicaraguans to complete a task. It is important to keep in mind though that it may be easy for some travelers in this type of program to consider their lives superior to those they are serving, perhaps inadvertently, equating economic privilege with superiority and poverty with inferiority. If you are considering serving on a trip like this

Nicaraguan experience, we recommend that you practice mind-fulness which allows you to recognize cultural similarities and differences without seeing one culture as superior over another.

PEACE CORPS

The Peace Corps is a program, run by the US Federal Government, that places volunteers in countries around the world. Volunteers work in agriculture, community economic development, education, environment, health, or youth development.[6] Applicants can either apply for specific placements or at-large. Once accepted, they undergo an extensive months-long training session in-country, followed by a two-year term in their position, which can be renewed in many cases.[7]

In preparation to write this section, we spoke with Dr. Michael Foster who was a Peace Corps volunteer after completing his undergraduate degree. We include his personal experience because it is indicative of the type of experience you may have if you were to participate in the Peace Corps. Michael worked as an English teacher in a secondary school in Madagascar. Upon arrival in Madagascar, he received extensive training to prepare him to be a classroom teacher, a credential he did not gain in the United States. He said the training was effective in preparing him to do his job. As mentioned earlier, he also lived with a host family for a few months so that he could gain linguistic proficiency in Malagasy and cultural immersion. Because of this time dedicated to becoming a member of the local community, he attained a higher-than-anticipated proficiency in Malagasy. In addition to effective training, he also found the financial and logistical support provided by the Peace Corps to be good. They helped him find a place to live and paid him a stipend that exceeded what most local people made. Michael very much values his experience in the Peace Corps because it gave him the chance to confirm that he wanted to have a career in which he could teach and work with people who spoke different languages and who came from a variety of cultures.

OTHER WORK

The contents of this chapter are not meant to be an exhaustive list of ideas for study abroad-like experiences after finishing an undergraduate degree. There is work to be done with religious, charitable, professional, and other organizations that can take adults abroad in much of the same way the program we showcase here does. If you are interested and able to do so, we recommend that you think about what you want to get from an experience abroad and look around for a way to do it. You can utilize the advice given to undergraduates throughout this book and apply it to the unique situations found later in life.

CHAPTER 8

Getting the Most Out of Being There

TOURIST VERSUS SOJOURNER

When you think about traveling to another country, you may start out thinking a lot about all the famous sites you'll visit, the classic experiences you'll have, or the signature foods you want to eat. Understandably, you'll want to have many of the more well-known experiences that you've always associated with that place. Nonetheless, as someone who is going abroad for an extended time, you will want to make the shift from being a tourist on vacation to more of what we will refer to as a sojourner. Tourists sightsee (often as much as possible in the time they have), enjoy their vacation, take great photos for Instagram, eat fun foods, relax, explore the surface culture, and come home with souvenirs. On the other hand, sojourners recognize that this isn't a vacation, explore with purpose, experience a new way of life, build connections, find appreciation for the culture and the people of that culture, seek out meaningful interactions, get out of their comfort zone, and come home with a new perspective on life. It isn't that being a tourist and being a sojourner are mutually exclusive, there is an overlap between the two. The main difference lies in the approach to travel.

As an example, let's consider someone visiting Rome. A tourist will try to visit all the big sites: the Colosseum, the Roman Forum, the Trevi fountain, and the Sistine Chapel, eat pasta with red sauce (maybe even try to order spaghetti and meatballs, which is an American dish), and buy a t-shirt that says "Italia." A sojourner will get to know more about the city and explore sites with more detail. They learn that museums have a free day once a month and they take the time to appreciate various vast art collections across Rome. A sojourner will discover which restaurant makes the best *cacio e pepe bucatini*, Rome's signature pasta dish, and will try to find out which bars in the Trastevere neighborhood offer the best *aperitivo* (a drink and snacks) in the evening. Likewise, a sojourner will enjoy shopping at various markets, such as the Mercato Monti or Porta Portese, for special finds as mementos of their travels.

Since you have more time than the average person on vacation, you will learn more about famous sites and other lesser-known places. You might take a course on the history of the area (for credit or for fun), participate in local personalized tours, or speak to the docents at sites who can give you more information about what you are seeing. If you are studying abroad, some of these types of activities may be available to you as an international student, often for a discount or even for free. If you are working abroad, you might check with local coworkers about places they recommend that you see or any activities they highly suggest you do. Sometimes they may even offer to take you there themselves.

Also, with the additional time that you have in the country, you should remember that you don't have to see as much as you can as fast as you can. There is an inherent desire to do this as soon as you arrive, but this is a good way to experience tourism fatigue. If you are seeing too much too quickly, it all begins to blend, and you will find that you aren't able to appreciate the individual places very well. You'll also likely be very physically tired as well! Sightseeing frequently means walking and standing a lot, often on historic structures that aren't always very comfortable. (Do remember to pack great walking shoes!) Even if you're in amazing shape, it can tire you out faster than you think due to potential time changes and different climates. Remember that one of the great benefits of traveling for an extended period is that you can savor the sights and spread out your visits to them across the entire time that you'll be abroad. Consider making a general plan of the places you want to be sure to see at the beginning of your journey or even before you depart. Think through how you might schedule them across your stay. You'll want to be flexible, as there are sure to be new ones that you'll add to your list as you learn more about the community.

Being a sojourner doesn't mean you can't have the touristy experiences. You absolutely can and should do the things you are excited to do. Nonetheless, to get the most out of being there, we encourage you to take your experience further to allow for a more meaningful time.

GETTING INVOLVED

Another aspect of being a sojourner and getting the most out of living abroad is finding ways to become part of your new community. Making friends and finding regular activities to do will make your time abroad much more enjoyable and often more significant. In investigations into study abroad, several researchers have observed that students who create a local social network are the ones who report having higher levels of personal enjoyment or personal growth during their stay.[1] In interviews with students, both Melanie and Josh have also seen that people who report having the best experiences are those who found their friend group and regularly interacted with them while abroad. This is probably not surprising to you, but at the same time you might find yourself at a bit of a loss as to how to get started in building that new network of friends.

Rather than trying to make friends right away when you get there with whoever you happen to meet, you can try instead to put yourself in the position of opportunities for interaction with other people. As we mentioned in chapter 5, one of the best ways to do this is to find an activity that you can do regularly. A nice aspect of studying and living abroad is that you will discover that you have more free time available to you because you aren't doing all the same activities and chores that you have at home. This extra time can allow you to look for groups that align with your interests or that offer something new to you based on things you'd like to explore. Often these types of activities can be special ones that are unique to the country or area. While campus life abroad is different than US college campuses, you will discover that there are still activities and interest groups around. There might not be an activities fair on the quad like at your US institution, but that doesn't mean you can't find these groups. Look around for bulletin boards (physical and virtual), join school-related social media accounts, and ask around for where you might find information about groups (the international student office). Also, consider looking outside the school, in the local community for opportunities too. In some ways you may need to make some extra effort to find these types of activities, but once you do, it will be worth the effort. If you are not attending school abroad, you might ask coworkers or neighbors for information about local groups or activities.

When choosing activities, there are a couple of things to consider. First, if your goal is to make friends, you want to choose something that allows for some type of conversation or interaction with others. Say, for example, you decide to join a sports group. You will probably have opportunities to get to know people before and after the games and practices, but there won't be time to chat during play. This might mean you need to plan to get there a bit early or leave a bit late so you can maximize your interaction time. But let's say instead you decide to join a tandem language conversation partner group. Since the goal of tandem partners is to converse in your two languages (half the time in your first language, and half the time in your second), you will have ample time that is dedicated to talking to someone else. This is also a great way to practice and learn more of your second language if you are in a non-English-speaking country.

Through her research into study abroad at a variety of locations, Melanie found several participants had a variety of activities that helped them meet local people and other people with shared interests. Here is a list of these activities that can help give you ideas. Keep in mind that this is not an exhaustive list, but simply one to help you generate ideas.

- informal sports or fitness groups
- fun noncredit class (cooking, wine tasting, art, dance)
- tandem language partners
- volunteering (school, museum, health center, animal shelter, orphanage, church, EFL tutoring)
- informal performing groups (choir, dance, acting)
- trivia group
- Bible study
- nature walk group
- board game or card game group

Another aspect to consider when deciding to participate in an ongoing activity is your enjoyment of said activity and how likely you are to commit yourself to it. While these activities should allow you to meet people, they should also provide you with a fun hobby to enjoy outside of your classes or your work. For that to happen, you need to choose something that you feel you will want to keep doing and something that will allow you to make a real commitment to the group. If you are only able to attend sporadically, your chances of meeting people will decrease and people will be less likely to want to get to know you because they don't know if you will be around. If, for example, the group always meets on Saturday morning, but you know you'll be traveling a lot of weekends, it might not be worth it to join. Additionally, while you may want to try new activities during your time abroad, you also want to be sure that you are choosing something that you have a high likelihood of enjoying. Say, for example, you've always wanted to learn more about cooking and have some experience cooking for yourself, you might find that a once-a-week cooking class about local cuisine is an enjoyable activity that you can easily return to each week. However, if you've never cooked before or don't have any interest in cooking, you might become disillusioned with the class fairly quickly and end up bailing on it. For any new activity, it is important to give it a real chance before you decide to leave. Remember that you will not be perfect at something new right away, and in many cases, it won't matter how "well" you do at the activity as long as you are enjoying it. If you do decide to leave a group, it is courteous to tell the group leader or organizer so that they know not to expect you in the future.

A third aspect to consider when joining an activity group is to not worry about doing it with someone you know. Often people may hold themselves back from being more independent while abroad. We know a student who was so insistent that she had to do things with her roommate that she often found herself participating in activities she didn't like and missing out on other activities that she wanted to do but her roommate didn't. At first it may seem too intimidating to do things all on your own and you might feel that you need to participate in activities where you at least know one person. Nonetheless, we strongly encourage you to take the bigger step to be more independent and try new experiences based on your own interests and not based on who or who won't be there with you. Remember that you have already taken a big step in going abroad, probably on your own, and so you can make another smaller step in joining groups by yourself.

MAKING FRIENDS

It has probably been a while since you thought about how to make friends and what it takes to sustain a friendship. When going abroad, it's a good idea to spend some time considering these aspects because making friends in a new country can be more challenging than it is in your home community. (This is not to say that making friends at home is easy either!) A key aspect to remember is that friendship takes effort, planning, and reciprocation. Please understand though as a newcomer to a community, there is typically more onus on you to make a friendship successful.

In their research, Melanie and Josh have seen that many people who go abroad have a sense that friendships just "happen" and that if they aren't successful in making friends it is just because it never "happened" for them. This is a passive approach to take when trying to make friends and more often than not it leads to less success at finding friendships. If you want a better shot at getting to know people in your host country and creating lasting friendships, we suggest taking a more proactive approach. This means being more open to the idea of meeting people and becoming friends to spend time together. This might mean being the first person to speak up and introduce yourself, or it could mean spending time in situations where you are more likely to meet people. This can be hard if you are more introverted or prefer to let others make the first move. It's a good idea though to consider this a chance to try something different from your usual routine, much in the same way you are trying new cultural or social actions.

This also usually means taking the initiative to make the plans for activities together. As mentioned, especially if you are making friends with a local person, as a foreigner, you usually need to show a greater level of commitment and interest in the friendship. This does not mean you have to come on strong or in a pushy manner, but just that you need to show sufficient enthusiasm so that the person will know you are sincere. In areas that are popular for study abroad or that may have many foreign visitors, a local person may have tried making friends with foreigners before only to find out that the person didn't want to commit to the friendship. A student studying in San José, Costa Rica, told us that he had no trouble meeting local students but that often they seemed wary about making plans with him because they were so used to foreign students flaking out and ghosting them. He said when he first started suggesting plans and showing up, the locals were genuinely surprised and pleased. For him, just those initial times of being committed to plans were enough for his new friends to realize he was serious about getting to know them and he ended up becoming close with several local people.

Part of building and sustaining friendships means making sufficient time for other people. This might be when you have to fight against some touristy feelings and remember that locals might not want to visit famous landmarks or museums with you all the time. This will also mean planning to spend time in your local community when you have time off. After all, if you are away traveling to other places frequently, you will have less time to be with local friends. Spending time with friends at a local place for a few hours just hanging out might seem like you're not doing enough to take advantage of "being there," but chances are, you are doing exactly what locals do. Remember that sometimes the smaller, less exotic moments might end up being the ones that help you experience the culture and way of life in your host country. When Melanie was studying in Italy, her favorite times ended up being the countless hours she spent with friends in different piazzas around Rome, enjoying a drink or some food, and simply chatting. These weren't famous piazzas or fancy, memorable restaurants, but they were authentic Italian experiences that she shared with her new local friends.

Another aspect of making friends is trying out new activities that you might not typically do. Again, this is similar to other cultural aspects that you will be exposed to while abroad. We recommend adopting a "say yes" policy to help you try out new things and to help you with your new friendships. The idea of this is to keep an open mind and to discover new experiences. This might mean trying out something that you wouldn't normally do on your own or that isn't part of your usual routine. You might find that you enjoy this new activity and can become closer to a new friend because you decided to go outside your comfort zone. Nonetheless, you should not put yourself in situations where you feel unsafe or where you know you will not enjoy the activity. We encourage you to be open to new experiences but not to be in a situation that will make you miserable or worse.

When considering the reciprocation part of friendship, a note should be made about being a good communicator. While there are language differences to consider (discussed in more detail next), someone who is easy to contact and who responds promptly is more likely to be successful at making friends. We understand that no one wants to be tied to their phone, but when making new friends, it is important to answer messages or phone calls to stay engaged in the friendship. It's probably not much of a surprise that students who reported being "bad at texting" or stating that they "were lazy about texting back" were those who struggled to make friends abroad. Again, this is part of putting in effort to show that you are serious about being someone's friend. It is also important to use the messaging apps that are common in the host country. For example, in many places people use WhatsApp instead of the standard text messaging app that comes with the phone. This is usually because it is cheaper to use data than to send SMS texts abroad. When asking new friends for their contact information, it's always a good idea to confirm what apps they like to use.

If you are in a non-English-speaking community, your ability to make friends might be influenced by your language skills. Generally, it is easier for more advanced second language speakers to make native speaker friends because they can have higher quality conversations about a variety of topics. Nevertheless, even lower-level speakers can find ways to make friends with locals. Plus, chances are that if you can interact with local friends you will improve your language skills more than by only taking classes.[2] A good way to assist you in making local friends is to consider activities that are designed for local people to interact with English speakers or foreigners. The people who choose to participate in those types of groups or activities are usually more open to foreigners and typically more sensitive to non-native speakers. Likewise, if your new friends want to speak English with you, it helps if you are extra sensitive to the fact that they are trying to communicate in their second language too.

You will probably also have opportunities to make friends with other foreigners studying and living abroad. It will be easy to bond over your shared experience of being in a new situation even when you might come from different backgrounds. In some ways you might even find it easier to get to know other foreigners instead of locals since they are also looking to make new friends. This is also usually a good way to get to know others who might have similar language skills to yours and where you can feel more comfortable trying to speak in your second language. Chances are high too that other foreigners speak English which can take away some of the burden of communication for you. But again, we remind you to be kind about their language skills in English as it may be another second language for them. Remember it takes commitment to sustain these friendships and it helps if you are proactive, similar to how you might be with locals.

GETTING THE MOST OUT OF CONVERSATIONS ABROAD

As language instructors and language learners, both Josh and Melanie have experienced the ups and downs of conversations in other languages. To assist you with conversations in your second language either with native speakers or other non-native speakers, we have four general tips for you. The first tip is to be aware of the conversation structure. In general, conversations have greetings, opening talk (small talk), the main point, pre-closing talk, and a closing greeting.[3] This is not something we think about in our first language because we are so accustomed to having conversations. Yet, as second language speakers we tend to skip over parts of conversation because we are so focused on the main point. We also have to be aware that different languages may approach conversation structure differently.[4] For example, some languages may have more elaborate greeting structures.[5] This is part of the language learning process that you generally observe through having conversations. Simply being more aware of this, and trying to notice how native speakers handle these parts of conversation will help you to improve your own conversation skills.

The second tip is to find ways to show that you are listening and engaged in the conversation. A good way to do this is to learn the little response sayings or words that people use in the language to demonstrate listening. Do not rely solely on the word "yes" as this can become very repetitive and can often be mistaken as someone who does not understand the conversation or is not listening. Pay attention to facial expressions and gestures too as these can be indicative of whether or not someone is interested in a conversation. Again, this may take some time to observe as it is not typically part of standard language lessons. Some ways to do this on your own before you go abroad can be through watching or listening to conversations between native speakers on talk shows or podcasts. Usually, the host of the show will be interviewing a guest and they need to demonstrate that they are listening. These are good options because you can observe mostly spontaneous speech but in a fairly controlled environment that is designed for others to see or hear.

Third, you will want to make sure to practice asking questions. Questions are a useful strategy for clarifying information and for generating more conversation.[6] They will help you gain additional details and often may lead to the other person repeating information that will help you better understand the conversation. This preparation will include studying the main question words and the general structure of questions so that your conversation partner will know that you are asking a question. If you are at a lower level, we recommend you stick with the concrete questions of "Who?" "What?" "Where?" and "When?" as these provide concrete answers that are easier to understand. Asking "Why?" or "How?" can be very useful in generating conversation but the answers will be more complex and you might struggle to understand them. You can also ask yes/no questions, which are good for clarification, but be aware that these are often short answers that do not generate more talk. In part of studying questions, you should also consider what possible answers you will receive. One of the conundrums of language teaching is the famous question "Where is the bathroom?" This is naturally an important question, but it is often taught well before the words and phrases for directions, and as such, most beginners don't comprehend the response. So, as part of your questions, be sure to practice the answers too.

Our final tip is related to practicing questions as we recommend knowing different ways to ask for clarification. To do this, think about the various reasons why you might need clarification such as not hearing someone, not understanding a word, getting too much information at once, or needing the information more simply stated. The more specific you can be as to what type of clarification you need, the better help you will receive from the other speaker. For example, saying "Can you repeat that?" might result in getting the same sentence at the same pace. However, "Can you repeat that slower, with simple words?" will result in the other speaker altering their original sentence in an attempt to help you understand their meaning. As part of asking for clarification, you will want to be sure you know ways to tell the other person that you do or do not understand. The goal here is to maintain the conversation and to keep getting assistance if you need it. By affirming that you understood the clarification, the other person knows you can keep going with the conversation. Likewise, by sharing that you are still having difficulty understanding, the other person can try alternative methods to help you. In some cases, it might be too difficult to explain and that topic may have to be abandoned, but through asking for more information, you will have shown your interest in the topic and the conversation, which is encouraging when trying to build a friendship with others.

USING APPS TO MEET PEOPLE

In the relationship world, dating apps have become very commonly used as a means to meet other people. Recently, these apps have branched out to create friend-finding versions too that are rapidly growing in popularity.[7] These apps are also widely used overseas and often people going abroad for an extended period find them useful for meeting people. Granted most people are still using them for finding a romantic partner, which you could do, but as the use of these types of apps expands, you might find them a helpful tool for meeting locals for dating or friendship.

If you already have experience with these apps, you can easily update your information to your new location. (Although, be aware that the current app you prefer might not be used in your host country.) If you are new to apps like this, we recommend having a more experienced friend help you with the setup and creation of a profile. In both situations though you should be prepared for there to be cultural differences in the way the apps are used and how local people seek romantic partners. It is a good idea to do some research on dating apps and your host country before you go. It might mean making some adjustments to your profile so that you have a better chance of fitting in with the local culture, and thus find more success on the app. For example, in Japan, dating apps have a category for foreigners and while it may feel odd to think of yourself in that way, chances are you will have greater success at meeting people who are interested in meeting someone who isn't Japanese.

As mentioned earlier, you may need to take the first step in communicating with a potential new friend (or romantic interest) as a way to show that you are interested in getting to know the person. When making that first contact, try to ask a question about the person who will start off a conversation. While a simple "Hi" might seem like enough, it might feel like minimal effort to the other person and there's a good chance they won't think you're interested or even real. Apps like these are full of foreigners pretending to be interested in meeting up with locals (usually for some type of financial scam), and so you will want to try to make yourself appear as real as possible. This doesn't mean you have to come on strongly or send a whole bunch of messages right away. Something simple like "Hi! I'm here studying in [location] and I thought this app would be helpful in meeting people. I liked your profile. Is that your dog in the photo?" can be an effective way to start a conversation.

When using apps to meet friends, you should be aware of a few aspects. First, since these are branch-offs of dating apps, some people still use them to find romantic partners. This can be frustrating if you're not particularly interested in dating. Second, some apps will only let you find friends of the same gender identity. This is an attempt to cut down on the misuse for dating purposes, but it can limit your friendship possibilities. Third, as stated previously, as with any apps used for socialization, these apps can be filled with scammers and people trying to sell you things. Be aware of anyone that seems too good to be true or tries to get too close to you too fast. Likewise, never send money or gift cards to potential friends.

In addition to dating or friendship apps, other social media apps can also be useful for meeting local friends. Several apps, like Facebook, have dedicated groups for people in a certain region with a shared interest. Some of these groups have in-person events or meetings that are open to the public too. Often people like the aspect of getting to know people online first as a way to feel comfortable and break the ice, and then have the option of meeting in person at a group event.

When talking about meeting new people that you've met online, this is a good place to remind you about safety. When making plans to see each other in person, always plan to meet that person at a location where you know there will be plenty of other people around. Do not go to someone's home for a first meeting and do not have them pick you up at your home. Make sure you have your own transportation and have a backup option just in case. Tell another friend about your plans before going and text that person with an update at least once during your time out. If you don't know many local people, this might seem difficult but even checking in with a roommate or colleague can be helpful in case of an emergency. If you have something to eat or drink, pay close attention to your plate or glass and if you have to let either out of your sight, do not continue to eat or drink from it. It is also recommended that you go easy on drinking alcohol when meeting someone new, as having too much to drink can impair your decision-making. Finally, if you feel uncomfortable for whatever reason, leave. You do not owe the other person an explanation nor do you owe it to them to stay. If you feel as though you need assistance with leaving, try to alert someone working at the place. It is better to be overly cautious in situations where you have a bad feeling rather than to regret not making a safer choice when you had the opportunity.

In this chapter, we hope we've given you some ideas and strategies for how to get more involved in your new community and how to feel more engaged. Through our research and experiences, we've seen that people who make the effort to become part of the host community report having more meaningful experiences along with higher levels of cultural appreciation and greater levels of enjoyment during their time abroad. Nonetheless, it is up to you to decide what it will mean to you to get the most out of being in your chosen country. As we've suggested in earlier chapters, setting goals for your time abroad can help you consider what will be most important to you, just keep in mind that those goals may change as you experience more that your new community has to offer.

CHAPTER 9

Changing Identity Perspectives

STUDY ABROAD CHANGES A PERSON IN WAYS THAT CANNOT always be predicted. One major attraction to study abroad is also what can make it daunting: the unknown about what life in other countries will be like and what potential language and cultural barriers may make life uncomfortable. These challenges cause changes and force many people to learn about themselves. In this chapter, we discuss the concept of identity, how it relates to study abroad, and how the skills you learn during study abroad may change the way you perceive yourself.

WHAT DO WE MEAN BY IDENTITY?

Bonny Norton, a renowned researcher into the connections between identity and language learning, defined identity as "the way a person understands his or her relationship to the world, how that relationship is constructed across time and space, and how the person understands possibilities for the future."[1] This is the definition we use to guide how we discuss identity in study abroad in this chapter because we see its applications to study abroad, even if you aren't studying language. Let's dive into that definition. When you study abroad, you have the chance to "understand [your] relationship to the world . . . across time and space" when you begin noticing how being in your host country is changing how you perceive yourself and your skills. This will ultimately change the way you perceive your "possibilities for the future," as well. We will dig into these possibilities throughout this chapter. It is important to note that someone doesn't have just one identity. That would be like you only seeing yourself as a student. That's not the case at all nor should it be when you're thinking about how study abroad and identity are connected. We all have multiple identities that are connected to things like gender, sexual orientation, religion, linguistic experience, race, and ethnicity, among an infinite number of others. Even *Star Wars* fandom can be an identity. Study abroad may affect each of these differently.

To illustrate how study abroad and identity connect, let's take a look at a research study. Researchers Xingsong Shi and Xiaoyan Guo wrote about three adults from China who studied abroad in the United States as part of a graduate degree.[2] They were interested in how their participants' multiple identities influenced their approach to learning English during their time abroad and how that experience with English also affected their identities. Here, we mention a few relevant results from that study. First, there were two participants who, when they began their study abroad, perceived themselves as not having the linguistic proficiency needed to be identified as an English speaker, which they felt they needed for their professional lives. One of those two people sought out increased social interaction in English, realized that she didn't need to speak completely like a native speaker to be identified as an English speaker, and thus adapted the way she saw herself, as a competent English speaker. The other participant felt bogged down by various responsibilities given to him and he did not socialize in English as much, focusing more on his professional identity and less on his linguistic identity. Second, the third participant valued her identity as someone who had experienced a diversity of world cultures more than languages. Therefore, she spent her time traveling around the United States and exploring culture.

IDENTITY AS A WORLD CITIZEN

Before you begin to imagine what your changed identities may look like during and after study abroad, take some time to consider your identities at home. For most people, a study abroad experience is the first chance they have had to spend an extended period in another country. For some people, it may even be the first time they have left their home country, or even their home region. If this describes you, you are surely very familiar with how to live life in your area. You know how to buy groceries, move around your city, know the types of food you can have, and what the social norms are for interacting with other people in your area. If your exposure to life in other countries is limited to what you can observe on TV, in social media, or through other people's experiences, it may be surprising to encounter life in your host country. Those surprises may lead you to see yourself as someone who can move through different cultures, while becoming a member of multiple communities, and, ultimately, a world citizen. We'll take a look at what that can look like in the next sections of this chapter.

LEARNING TO NAVIGATE LIFE

Think about the steps you take when you go to the grocery store in your hometown. When you are getting ready to leave your house, you dress in what you know is culturally acceptable clothing for your area. When you leave, you lock your door and make your way to your familiar transportation mode, let's say, for example, your car. You probably don't have to think too much about how to drive your car and navigate streets to get to the grocery store. Once you're inside, you understand the order you do things. You likely will get a cart, pick up your items, and head to the cash register. You know what kinds of interactions to expect with store employees who assist you in checking out. You know how to pay and to carry your groceries away.

You may be wondering why we just wrote a paragraph about how we go to the grocery store in many parts of the United States. It's because it is a very familiar process to so many people and you might not expect it to be different when you arrive in your host country. However, it may very well be quite different. Go back to the process that we just went through. When you're getting ready to go to the grocery store, you may need to dress differently than you would in the United States as you strive to fit in with local customs. Your transportation may be different since almost no one has a car with them during study abroad. Walking or using public transportation is much more likely the way you'll go. When you get to the grocery store, you may find surprises. For example, you may find products you've never seen before, like native fruits and vegetables, meats and fish (and the smells that go with them!), and products you can't figure out. You may find that products are in unexpected locations, for example, the eggs aren't in a refrigerated section. The actions you're expected to know to do may be different. You may have to weigh your produce before going to the cash register. You may need to request and pay for a bag for your groceries (unless you brought one with you—a good idea to do!). You may find that store employees do not expect to interact with you. You may even find that you can't get everything in one store. There are surely surprises that we can't even anticipate that you may encounter during your shopping trip.

This hypothetical grocery store visit is an important example of learning to navigate life in your host country and becoming a world citizen. You undoubtedly already know that you'll need to learn how to live in your host country. Even with that, there will be surprises. For example, before studying abroad in Spain, Josh knew that he would have to eat meals later than he was accustomed to in the United States. What he didn't realize was that that also meant that family time with his host family would also be much later since they liked to watch TV together.

LEARNING TO TRY NEW THINGS

Some people have personalities that lend themselves to being adventurous when it comes to trying new things. Other people have a harder time with this. From our experience as students, professors, and researchers in study abroad, we know for a fact that those who see themselves as capable of trying new things during study abroad many times have more positive experiences and are happier with their experiences. Frequently, this manifests itself around the dinner table since local food and related customs are where there will be many cultural differences. To illustrate, we'll use the example of when Josh accompanied a group of fifteen university students to Spain and Portugal in 2019. Many students in this group had been reluctant to eat Spanish food, in particular seafood, a staple in the region they were in. Group meals frequently became a stressful event for the group because of the lack of willingness to try new things. So, when one night the trip leaders were told that the group would be served tuna stew, they got nervous. Finally, one of Josh's colleagues determined that they weren't going to tell the students what they were eating. It worked! Especially since students were speculating that they were eating pork, the group was collectively much more willing to try and enjoy what they had been served. That same colleague even said she had had a student end up in the hospital because she refused to try new foods for four days on a university trip to Thailand.

In addition to food, it is quite probable that you will encounter and be asked to participate in cultural practices that are new to you. These may include different daily schedules and different types of relationships between family members, between student and instructor, among others. If you find yourself in an unfamiliar situation, such as in a course where the instructor teaches differently than you're accustomed to, work on trying to see what could be good in that practice. Give it a try and it may be all right. Furthermore, you may encounter a cultural practice that contradicts an important aspect of your identity. These may or may not include practices related to religion, gender, and LGBTQ+ status, among others. While we are definitely not advocating for you to give up an important part of how you see yourself, it is important to reflect on the cultural differences associated with these practices.

Since the essence of study abroad is living in a new environment, you will be faced with situations that resemble that of Josh's students in some way. There will be unfamiliar foods. There will be new ways of doing things that you would normally do at home. It may be daunting but we strongly recommend that you work on being someone who can try the unfamiliar. If you don't like it, you don't always have to repeat it but at least you tried it.

LEARNING TO INTERACT WITH A DIVERSE GROUP OF PEOPLE

During many study abroad experiences, students find they interact with a wider variety of people than they had expected prior to departure. For example, if you are an international student studying in Australia, you can definitely expect to encounter students from other countries, such as Japan. It is even possible that you may develop strong friendships with those international students from other countries. This happened to Josh in Spain when one of the people he stayed in contact with most after study abroad was from Mexico. Similarly, in her interviews with study abroad students, Melanie also found that many students reported making close friendships with other international students from several countries. They reported that while these other students had very different cultures, they shared the experience of navigating the host country's culture together. Just like your encounters with new types of cultural practices and ways to navigate life, you will likely meet people with different experiences from you. You need to focus on seeing yourself as someone who can interact with people from a variety of backgrounds, figure out how to spend time together and learn from each other.

Even though you've been reading about how different people you encounter will be when compared to your experiences at home, don't forget that there will be similarities that will be important to notice. Your host community will still be a heterogeneous population, just like the one you come from. There will be people who are extroverts and introverts, artistic and analytical, and any other types of distinctions you could make.

UNDERSTANDING THE WORLD AND YOUR PLACE IN IT

Through your conversations with people you meet during your time abroad, the new experiences you undergo, and the observation and practice of various cultural norms, you may find that you start seeing the world differently. This will likely mean also seeing how you and your home community fit in the world differently. For example, go back to the Japanese students that you met while studying abroad in Australia. Through your interactions with the Japanese students and the Australian people that you meet, you will be exposed to practices that will make you see how people from three different countries perceive the world. It will make you alter the way you think about where you fit. Perhaps you may even feel a little bit Japanese or a little bit Australian. You may see the way you used to do things back at home as the "odd way," perhaps even negatively. Reconciling these new perspectives with your past is an important part of study abroad and should be something that you reflect on.

NEW SKILLS THAT AFFECT HOW YOU SEE YOURSELF

In addition to new experiences that will allow you to form a new image of how you view yourself during study abroad, you will also learn many new skills that may also alter the way you perceive your multiple identities. While the exact combination of skills will be individualized, some of the most common skills that are learned through study abroad, beyond linguistic and intercultural proficiencies, are independence, flexibility, and problem-solving. We will take a look at each of them in this section.

INDEPENDENCE

For many people, study abroad may be the first time they are separated from their families and friends in the United States. This type of separation may not only be based on mileage but it could also be based on time zones. Imagine that you're studying abroad in India and your family is in the Central Time Zone in the United States. You're going to be close to twelve hours ahead of your family back home. If you are used to running your thoughts and decisions by your family and friends through text messages every day, you will have to change this behavior unless you want to wake up someone.

Study abroad leads to independence from Day One, especially if you are traveling by yourself to your host country. This can be daunting if you have never traveled by air or been through customs before. You will survive this though. You will make it to your host country, usually without major issues. Once you've accomplished that, you've already navigated a difficult challenge if you're used to depending on other people. This growth in independence may continue to become more pronounced as you are forced to confront new linguistic and cultural challenges during your time abroad. Some of this may be through travel. Although he already felt independent, Josh grew in independence during his ten-day solo trip to Greece over Holy Week during his study abroad year. The fact that he figured out what to do when the regional bus he was traveling on pulled over along the side of the highway without warning and everyone started getting off the bus, shows the fruit of his increased independence. It was a big teaching moment in how you assess a situation, and ask for help as it's available so that you can safely get yourself through a problem (and he did!).

FLEXIBILITY

We once became familiar with a student named Courtney (a pseudonym since she was a research participant). Courtney was a native speaker of English, studying abroad in Spain. What made Courtney unique was that she was also a heritage speaker of Finnish, meaning that she had a parent who was from Finland and spoke with her in Finnish in their home in the United States. Courtney spent a considerable amount of time in Finland as a teenager without other members of her American family. While there, she encountered numerous situations of culture shock and surprise that taught her to be more flexible. She brought these lessons and applied them to her time in Spain. We bring up Courtney in this context because her change in flexibility ended up being something that made a difference in how she saw herself. When she compared how she saw herself before and after her international experiences, she saw herself as a much more flexible person who was able to deal with ambiguity and surprises.[3]

This is important in study abroad. If you are studying abroad in a country where one of your native languages isn't a prominent language, you may find yourself not understanding a lot of what you are seeing and hearing. With some practice, you should work to become more accustomed and willing to accept that you will not understand all of the words you hear. You will quickly find that you still find ways to go about your life. For instance, you may not learn all of the German words on signs in the Berlin U-Bahn but you will learn to identify keywords you need to navigate through that subway system.

Related, go back to that grocery store we mentioned earlier in this chapter. You will probably have a better experience in a foreign grocery store if you also learn to be flexible in cultural practices related to shopping. For instance, be flexible and don't assume your cashier is rude if they don't make small talk with you. Being flexible like this may allow you to find that you question the cultural practices in your home community, especially after you become familiar with your host country's way of doing that task. You may ask yourself which way is the best way to do it and why. Should the cashier make small talk with the customer or not? Do you view a talkative cashier as friendly or do you view a quiet cashier that will answer questions if you have them as someone who is there to do a job? One way isn't better than the other. They are just different. The point here is that being flexible will allow you to experience new perspectives that may ultimately change the way you view or move through the world.

PROBLEM-SOLVING

While you become more independent and flexible, you are practicing important problem-solving skills, which will help you see yourself as an educated member of society. If you are skilled at problem-solving, you are good at identifying a problem, assessing its need and importance accurately, identifying and weighing your options, and enacting the best solution to your problem. Place yourself as someone who is studying abroad in Mexico. In many Mexican cities, it is common to use city buses as transportation. Imagine you are riding the bus, you see that you are a couple of blocks from your stop, and you watch for the bus to get to your stop. The problem is that the bus doesn't stop where you expect since it has a slightly different route going in the opposite direction. Now, with each passing minute, you are getting farther and farther from where you were supposed to go. What do you do? Do you identify this problem as one that you need to act on? What are your possible solutions? Do you talk to the driver, or to other passengers? Do you wait until you get to the end of the route assuming the bus will turn around?

Working through a situation like this in an environment in which you don't have a native intuition on how to do things or how to express yourself linguistically, can be scary but it can also teach you how to solve a problem like this. For the record, Josh went with the last option. It was not the right one. He lucked out that the driver walked him over to another bus that took him back to the hotel he was staying at.

WHAT IS HAPPENING AT HOME?

While you are abroad becoming a more independent, flexible, problem-solving world citizen, your communities at home are continuing with their own lives. You can't expect your family members and friends to not get out and do things while you're gone. This creates a situation in which you are forming new experiences, new realities, and new aspects of your identity, and they are also doing the same. You and your family and friends are on divergent paths. You may see evidence of these divergent paths on social media, leading you to feel you are missing out on what is happening at home, and causing homesickness to settle in. Now, don't panic. This doesn't mean that your relationship with them is over. You will just need to work to figure out how your post-study abroad self mixes with the community at home.

"How was your trip?"

Your family and friends were not with you during your study abroad. This is good! However, this also means that it is not possible for them to fully understand what your experiences have been like. If they also studied abroad, they may have an idea of what happened during your sojourn but they can't understand your entire experience. You need to realize that someone who has never studied abroad or someone who has never traveled much may be very interested in what you have been doing but may need a patient explanation. Imagine that you have just returned from a semester abroad and someone asks you, "How was your trip?" Your first reaction may be to say, "I didn't take a trip," since you may see a semester abroad as much more than a trip in the vacation sense. This can be a good opportunity to be patient and tell people what study abroad can be like. Show them photos and tell them stories that reflect the reasons why you see your experience as much more than just a trip. Tell them about the work that you did in class, the people you formed relationships with, and how you see yourself as a changed person.

REVERSE CULTURE SHOCK

As we discussed in chapter 4, when you first arrive in your host country at the beginning of your study abroad experience, and throughout your stay, you will undoubtedly experience culture shock, feeling some kind of discomfort, disorientation, or surprise about a difference between the host country and your home. You have surely anticipated this kind of culture shock. However, what many people don't consider as much is reverse culture shock. This happens when you return home. If you are returning to life in the United States, you may find aspects of life to be surprising or disorienting. You may even see US life as inferior to your host country. For example, when Josh returned to Missouri from his academic year in Spain, he found it very odd that he needed to use a car to get places as opposed to walking or using public transportation. He also found aspects of social life in the United States to be inferior to what he experienced in Europe. Similarly, a student we know spent a year in Japan, and upon returning home, found the public systems and general way of life in the United States to feel out of date and technologically inferior. In his first months back home, he was frequently frustrated by American systems that he felt could be handled so much better if only we were to use a Japanese approach.

Even though most people who return from study abroad are excited to see friends and family they haven't seen in a long time, it's also normal for them to experience these feelings of reverse culture shock. This reverse culture shock may mean you are experiencing certain emotions. While you are excited to see family, you may be missing your host country and the people you met there. This makes sense since you probably bonded with your classmates, host family, conversation partners, and other people during your time abroad. You may find yourself especially missing classmates since they have experienced and are experiencing something like you are. You may also miss some of the freedom and independence you had while abroad. You may have spent weeks or even months making your own decisions only now to be back home with family and close friends where you must consider their input on decision making.

Reconciling Your Post–Study Abroad Self into Your Home Life

You will not be able to avoid the reality that you have changed since you left for study abroad and the people you know at home have also changed during that time in different ways. This is not necessarily a bad thing. Part of what makes study abroad so valuable is learning to merge your new self into your home life. To do so, we recommend you do a few things. First, stay connected to your host country in some way. Hopefully, you established some contacts that you can send messages to regularly. You can also keep up with current events in that country through online news. Second, make sure to value the people in your home life. Talk openly about what all of you experienced during the time you were away in a way that doesn't make either experience better than the other. This will allow you to introduce your new self to them and will also allow them to catch you up. Third, don't rush through processing your return. It will take you some time to reacclimate to home life. Stay in touch with the people you studied abroad with and talk about your common experiences in this readjustment.

Identity is complex and complicated. It may take you a long time to really appreciate how study abroad may have changed the way you perceive yourself and your skills. You may even be confused or unhappy with your changes and may need help in processing them. Be patient with yourself as you work through your experiences.

Chapter 10

Study Abroad and Your Career

As you plan for your study abroad, you should consider the impact study/travel abroad can have on your career and your success in landing a great job. Even if you don't see the connection between your reasons for wanting to go abroad and your career, many applicable aspects of your time abroad can be beneficial to you in your work. The skills you gain during an experience abroad are skills that employers value and having these skills can help you stand apart from the crowd of prospective employees. While the number of American students abroad has shown a strong increase for decades, less than 2 percent of college students participate in study abroad.[1] (This percentage is taken from the 2019 data, as total numbers were lower for the 2020–2021 and 2021–2022 academic years due to continued COVID-19 restrictions for travel.) While this alone will make you unique, there are ways to make your study abroad more influential toward your future career. Rather than having study abroad as one line on your resume or CV, finding ways to mention your time abroad throughout the job-seeking process can provide you with opportunities to showcase what you learned while participating in that unique experience. Furthermore, remembering the lessons you learned (both formal and informal) will serve you well in your job.

Being Career-Minded while Abroad

As part of planning your experience abroad, we suggest you consider your career goals as part of that preparation. If you are participating in an academic program, you should look to see if there are unique career-focused courses you might be able to take while in the country. Many programs offer classes that focus on local businesses or international businesses in the region. Some programs provide language courses that are specific to a particular career field such as healthcare, government, or law. Some courses provide more hands-on opportunities such as field trips or volunteer activities that allow you to use what you have learned in the community. An excellent example of this type of program can be found at Florence University of the Arts in Florence, Italy.[2] This school offers a variety of experiential career learning through courses that allow students to work at various local businesses such as a restaurant, clothing store, design company, pastry shop, community center, spa, and more. Students have opportunities to participate in several different positions at these businesses, providing them with a multitude of career skills that can be transferred to any number of careers in the future. Additionally, students in these programs benefit from faculty mentorship and oversight to help ensure a successful experience.

Another possible way to connect with careers while you are abroad is through internships. Some study abroad programs have internship experiences available that can often be taken for college credit instead of a class. These internships are a good option for you as they have already been selected as those who are looking for foreign students to work at their businesses. It is also possible to find study abroad programs that have a built-in internship as part of the program. For example, the Business Internship summer program in Valparaíso & Viña Del Mar, Chile from International Studies Abroad by WorldStrides provides students with an internship at a local business that has been arranged through the host institution.[3] You can also look for internships on your own through career sites or at local businesses. However, you should be aware that you may not be permitted to work in certain areas due to local laws regarding international employees, even if the internship is unpaid. You should also be aware that in non-English-speaking countries some internships require more advanced language skills in the local language. However, it is also common for companies to seek out native English speakers as interns to help boost their English-speaking capabilities or knowledge at the company.

As English is currently the most widely spoken language for international business, your status as a native or near-native English speaker can provide you with an advantage for international jobs. Nonetheless, it is beneficial to have a sense of which industries or companies appear to have the greatest need for international employees or native English speakers. While you are abroad, you should take note of which industries seem to be expanding in the region and those that appear to be successful there. You may find that certain businesses have more interest or need someone who has knowledge of the American market and the local market. Likewise, you might find US companies that are present in the local region that may be interested in hiring someone from the United States who has also spent time in the country and is familiar with potential local customers and their needs. It is also important to recognize that for certain businesses and regions, your importance as a native English speaker may not be as valued as in other areas. Consider Denmark where English is widely spoken. The Danish people might not see your native speaker status as overly unique or desirable as they pride themselves on speaking English very well already. Contrast this with South Korea where native English speakers are often sought out for positions particularly when the person appears to be from the United States.

In addition to internships or paid jobs, you might also consider a volunteer position that can allow you to gain additional career skills. Similar to at home, you can find many local orga-nizations that need volunteers. This is a great option if you are doing a shorter stay abroad, as volunteer commitments are usually for shorter periods or are less defined by a length of time than an internship or job. Additionally, most volunteer positions require minimal skills and will often provide you with training to com-plete the tasks that they need. Keep in mind the abilities you'll learn are usually those of entry-level positions, but they can still be beneficial in helping you build a resume. In interviews with stu-dents during various study abroad programs, Melanie found that students had participated in volunteering positions with schools, medical clinics, veterinary clinics, animal shelters, child care cen-ters, parks and recreation centers, food pantries, and museums. Some of these positions are directly related to students' career plans, for example, the student who planned to be a nurse and spent time doing patient intake with a medical clinic. While other positions more indirectly afforded students with an opportunity to improve career-based skills. One student shared how volunteer-ing as a docent in a museum provided her with a chance to work on her presentation skills and her professional communication making her feel more confident when interacting with strangers. It is a good idea to document your volunteer work while abroad. This can be accomplished in a variety of ways, such as journaling, and is useful in case you need to contact the organization again in the future. As a reminder, volunteering can also help you become more connected to the local community and can be a valuable way to make friends while abroad.

INCLUDING STUDY ABROAD IN YOUR CAREER MATERIALS

When creating your career materials such as a resume or CV, cover letter, portfolio, or other career documents, we highly rec-ommend that you include your study abroad experience. This may seem like an obvious step to you, but we have discovered that some students may be unsure of how to incorporate their study abroad in their career materials, while others do not remember to include it at all! Here we provide you with advice as to how to be sure to not only include your study abroad in your materials but also how to highlight your experience.

On your resume or CV you may choose to include your study abroad under your education or as a separate section after your education. To help potential employers know more about your experience, you should provide a brief description of your program, and your main activities while there. You can describe the type of coursework you completed or the general focus of your studies. The following are examples from both Melanie's and Josh's CV:

Universidad de Salamanca, Study Abroad, Spring Semester (January–June)
Spanish Language and Culture Program
Courses focused on Spanish communication, academic writing, art history, and literature. All courses were at an advanced level and two courses were taken with native speakers.

Bowling Green State University, Bowling Green, Ohio
Master of Arts in Spanish (coursework in language, literature, linguistics, and culture)

Universidad de Alcalá de Henares, Alcalá de Henares, Madrid, Spain
Academic year abroad in collaboration with BGSU
If you participated in an internship or volunteered during your study abroad, we suggest you list these separately from your study abroad program. You will want to include an internship under your work experience and list it as you would any other jobs you may have had. Be sure to include a clear description of your duties while there. You may also want to highlight any language or cultural skills that were pertinent to the internship. A volunteer

position can either go under work experience or in a section with other volunteer experience. Again, you will want to provide an explanation of the activities that you completed at the organization and include any language experience that you had while volunteering. With both internships and volunteer experiences, you might also choose to indicate the training you received while working there, especially training that appears relevant to your future career.

One of the best ways to highlight your study abroad experience is in your cover letter. While employers will expect you to write about your education in your cover letter, they are often looking for what made your learning special or unique, and this is where you have an opportunity to discuss your study abroad. Your resume is good for the summary of your program, but here in your letter you can emphasize certain aspects of your study abroad that allowed you to acquire knowledge you wouldn't have been likely to obtain had you remained at your home institution. This will also provide you with a chance to talk about the soft skills you acquired while studying abroad. Soft skills are those that deal with interpersonal communication, cultural knowledge and awareness, problem-solving, and overcoming adversity. As we mentioned in chapter 9, this is part of becoming a world citizen who can navigate different cultures and worldviews and is an excellent point to introduce to your future employer. We recommend including a concrete example of how your study abroad allowed you to improve in one of these areas. Incorporating an anecdote from your travels into your cover letter will make your letter more interesting to read and provide the potential employer with a better idea of who you are and make you a more memorable candidate. It's easier to remember the applicant who learned how to adapt to new social norms during their studies in Japan because they needed to learn how to greet others based on their social status than the applicant who wrote that they were "good at adapting to change." Here is a sample segment from a cover letter to illustrate our advice:

> Studying abroad in Rome provided me with a great opportunity to understand different cultures. At my school, I had classes with students from eight countries, and along with my daily interaction with Italian culture, I was able to experience these cultures' different perspectives on a variety of aspects. For example, I learned how my classmates each viewed time and the need to maintain a schedule. The Brazilian and Argentinian students, much like the Italians, had a rather relaxed view toward schedules and took start times for social events as a suggestion. Whereas, I found the Japanese and German students adhered to the schedules very strictly and were often frustrated or concerned if an event didn't start exactly when they expected. My experience taught me the importance of understanding different nationalities' expectations toward scheduling, which is a useful skill when working with a variety of international clients.

In this example, we provide a brief view of the applicant's study abroad program, which allowed interacting with a variety of cultures. We also include the example of time and scheduling because it is a concept that is often of great concern here in the United States for many career fields. By using a brief story like this one in your cover letter, you give the employer a chance to know more about how you have learned about other cultures in a manner that applies to their position and organization. This is also more memorable than simply stating that you "understand that different cultures view time differently."

As part of your career materials, we highly suggest having documentation of your study abroad. One of the best ways to do this is by having a copy of your international transcript. This is not typically something you can request directly from the school's website like you can at most US institutions. Additionally, as a temporary international student your records are likely handled differently than those of degree-seeking students. You should request your transcript through the office of international students at your host institution or your home school's study abroad office. Also, be aware that international transcripts usually take much longer to prepare than ones from US universities. You may not receive the transcript until a year after your study abroad. Due to this longer period, it is a good idea to have other documentation of your program as well. You can save copies of course syllabi, the acceptance paperwork from your application, other correspondence with the program, certificates of completion, copies of assignments, or any other document that can demonstrate the coursework you did while abroad. It is a good idea to begin saving these documents early on, as it may be difficult to find them later. Also, understand that you may have physical copies of these documents that you are responsible for keeping. Unlike the United States where most documents are digital and new copies can easily be requested, this is not always the case in other countries. The course completion certificate that you were given may be the only copy! An easy rule of thumb is to snap a photo of any documents as soon as you get them, as a potential backup.

DISCUSSING STUDY ABROAD IN AN INTERVIEW

During job interviews, you have plenty of opportunities to speak about your study abroad even if you were not directly asked about it. Consider classic interview questions that are likely to be used during interviews in a variety of fields. Questions that address problem-solving, overcoming difficulty, failure, decision-making, cultural or social awareness, and perseverance are all excellent opportunities to talk about what you experienced and learned during your study abroad. For example, consider the well-known question that asks you about a time you dealt with a difficult problem and how you solved it. A great way to answer this question would be to give a concrete example from your study abroad. A student Melanie interviewed about his experience told her about a time he got lost in the first week of his program in Spain. He needed to get back to his apartment, and he could have taken a taxi, but being on a limited budget, he didn't want to spend the money if he didn't have to. The student decided to see how well he could do by asking directions from locals in Spanish. At first, he was rather disheartened; the descriptions were so long he couldn't remember all the steps and sometimes he was confused by the vocabulary. But he persisted and would go as far as he could based on what he remembered and understood, then he would seek out another person and ask for more directions. It took him about an hour to get home, but through being determined and refusing to give up, he managed to understand enough to find his way home. The sense of pride in achievement that he felt was unmatched and it made him realize that even though it was difficult, he was glad he had kept trying. Now this story was originally told to Melanie as she interviewed students about what it was like to use their second language during study abroad. However, it is an excellent story to tell for the problem question because it shows that the candidate is not afraid to ask for help and will keep at a task until it is complete. While we hope that you have a successful study abroad experience, we also know that living and studying internationally means having to deal with unexpected issues. The memories of these issues can be a good way to highlight valuable life lessons that you gained that aren't as easy to articulate in a resume or cover letter.

Naturally, you can also focus on the positive aspects of your study abroad experience during your interview. Often you can provide shorter examples to support your main answers to a variety of questions. One of the most commonly asked questions in interviews is about your best attributes and greatest strengths. While most interviewees will simply state their three qualities and move on, a better option is to back up these qualities with an example or brief explanation. Say perhaps that you believe one of your greatest strengths is your adaptability to change. A good way to illustrate this is to explain how you adapted to a different lifestyle while abroad and the changes that you made to feel more connected to the culture. A student we know studied in South Korea for a semester and she learned how to adapt to the Korean ways of addressing different people based on social status. She found that while the general concept of honorifics was part of this process, there were also many other methods used to indicate status. The better she became at following native speaker practices, the more accepted she felt by native Koreans. Upon returning to the United States, she kept this awareness of social status in communication and she discovered that she could be a more effective conversationalist if she used some of the methods she learned in Korea with the norms we follow here.

If you are asked directly about your study abroad experience, one aspect to keep in mind is that you want to stand out and be memorable to the interviewer. An excellent way to do this is to focus on the unique elements of your study abroad rather than simply reporting that you studied in X location. It helps to highlight what courses you took, the special activities you did, and what you found to be most valuable about the experience. In particular, think about the aspects that would appeal most to potential employers. For example, you could speak about the coursework you did that had a career component, or you might mention that study abroad helped you to become more confident in decision-making. Even if you went to a very popular destination, consider something memorable that you could share with the interviewer. Remember that the goal of talking about study abroad during a job interview is to help the interviewer understand the skills that you gained during your time abroad and what you will be bringing to their organization.

Use Your Study Abroad Skills in Your Career

When you begin your new job, you can utilize your study abroad skills in your new workplace to help you acclimate to your position and your company. While there are a variety of skills that will be applicable, we will highlight four that we find to be the most germane to the situation of starting a new job: adapting to a new culture, being comfortable in an unfamiliar setting, asking for help, and learning the language.

You will discover that every organization has its own culture that is built upon the culture of the field, the community, and the larger network of other similar organizations. You may have experienced some of this culture already through your studies, but a lot of the elements will be new to you and have to be learned through experience. This is very similar to your study abroad destination. While you can read about the culture of the community you will visit, you will learn that you can only really start to understand that culture once you are there and become a part of it. As you start at your new company, school, or venture, keep in mind how you observed and began to participate in the culture while you were abroad. At the beginning of your stay abroad, you understood that you were an outsider and that you needed to be patient when understanding how things worked in your new country. The same applies to your new job. It takes time and effort to acknowledge how people relate to one another, how communication is handled, how participation is done during meetings, or even how lunch is taken. Rather than assume you already know how to function with your new colleagues, take the time to be the outsider and find your way to fitting in once you have a better sense of the general workday practices.

Part of studying abroad is learning how to deal with the sensations of being unsure or uncomfortable because everything is so new and so different. As we mentioned before, there will come a point in your time abroad where you feel that everything is incredibly strange. This is part of culture shock and you will learn how to accept those differences, and to deal with those feelings of uncertainty. When starting a new job, the same feelings will resurface. After the initial excitement of getting the job, meeting all the new people, and learning your responsibilities, you will reach a period of doubt where you may feel as though you don't know what you're doing or if this job is the right one for you. This is a normal feeling and one that happens to almost everyone. When you consider how you overcame these types of emotions during your study abroad, you will see that you can apply many of those same tactics here. Accepting that there will be times when you don't fully understand a situation is part of growing in your career. You will discover that there may be aspects of your job that you do not enjoy but must get through because they are a necessary part of your and your company's work.

As you learned early on during study abroad, there are times when you need to ask for help. You asked because you lacked the knowledge or because you weren't certain of how to do something in your new environment. This wasn't a sign of weakness nor did it give a negative impression of you; you were simply a person who needed assistance. It shows you are open-minded and teachable. One of the biggest mistakes that new employees make is not asking questions when they need help. Similar to your study abroad, you'll be in a new environment and there will be times when you don't have all the information you need. Again, just like with study abroad, asking questions does not reflect negatively on you. Instead, consider that asking questions is part of your normal, everyday activity, and that when you ask for help, you are more likely to complete the project correctly the first time. Chances are that as you become more established in your position, you will not need to ask for help as often. However, it is important to remember that everyone needs assistance from others from time to time. As you may have seen during your travels, it is still better to ask than to have the situation become a bigger issue later on that takes much more effort to solve.

If your travels took you to a non-English-speaking country, you were tasked with learning a second language to get by. While you may have only learned the basics, you still became sensitive to new words and labels, as well as new approaches to communication. Similarly, if you went to an English-speaking country, you encountered a new dialect with different norms from the English you speak at home. These language-learning skills are important to keep in mind as you begin a new position. While you will most likely be working in an environment where you are fully proficient in the community language, there will still be language elements that you will need to learn. There will be new vocabulary to learn based on the technical aspects of your job as well as new acronyms and jargon that people will use in your office. Consider how you learned new vocabulary while you were abroad, what strategies were you using then? Many of those same strategies can assist you here. Additionally, you will learn that different coworkers will employ their styles of communication that may differ greatly from yours. Depending on your field, you may be interacting more regularly with people from a variety of generations or backgrounds, and as such, you will start to be more accustomed to each group's style of speech. Think about how you learned to communicate with different groups of people during your study abroad. Chances are you can use many of the same techniques you used abroad at your job. Related to interacting with various groups of people, you will observe that different groups have a sense of what is considered polite and appropriate speech in a professional setting. While most workplaces will conform to the politeness standards of the larger community, you will find that there are often specialized types of polite language based on your new organization and your field. For example, in some fields using people's titles is expected, whereas in other fields it may be more common to address everyone by their first name. To be successful in learning the new politeness standards, use your observation skills from your study abroad. Reflect on how you were likely more sensitive to polite speech and how you worked to conform to appropriate language while abroad. When you bring that same energy to your workplace, you increase your chances of successful polite communication.

Much of what we learn and experience during a long-term stay abroad can be useful in our future careers. There are lessons that we carry with us for life that help us become more independent, mature, and socially savvy adults. Again, even if your travel abroad was not greatly career-focused, you will still have gained important capabilities that you can and should apply in your future career and personal life. Sometimes even small events that happened during our time abroad can have a larger impact in the future. As you share stories about those events and remember those moments when you discovered something new and different, you will find that knowledge valuable in your current life.

Final Notes

WE WOULD LIKE TO THANK YOU FOR TAKING THE TIME TO READ our book. We hope you enjoyed reading it and that you find our advice valuable for your time abroad. We wish you the very best of luck in your travels and we hope that your stay abroad is a memorable experience filled with all that you have dreamed of and more. If there is one final piece of advice we can give you, it is to know that your time spent abroad will be worth it. It will be unpredictable, delightful, anxious, fun, difficult, and spectacular, all of these things, but most of all it will be worth going.

Notes

Chapter 1

1. "Educational Travel and Education Tours Abroad," WorldStrides, accessed on September 8, 2023, worldstrides.com; "CIEE," accessed on September 8, 2023, ciee.org.

2. "ISEP Study Abroad," accessed on September 8, 2023, isepstudyabroad.org.

3. "Flamenco: Artistic and Cultural Expression," ISA Seville Study Center, accessed August 28, 2023,https://www.studiesabroad.com/destinations/europe /spain/seville/spanish-language-culture--business/isvu1124/flamenco-artistic -and-cultural-expression-562673.

4. "Summer Community Public Health," CIEE Santiago de los Caballeros, Dominican Republic, accessed September 5, 2023, https://www.ciee .org/go-abroad/college-study-abroad/programs/dominican-republic/santiago -de-los-caballeros/summer-community-public-health; "Study and Volunteer in Ghana," ISEP Direct, University of Ghana, accessed September 5, 2023, https://search.isepstudyabroad.org/Program/Detail/fc1a6b13-07d7-4445-a487 -2672676bd51c?ProgramTypeId=2.

5. "Gilman Scholarship Program," Benjamin A. Gilman International Scholarship, accessed September 8, 2023, gilmanscholarship.org.

Chapter 2

1. "How to Apply," US Department of State Bureau of Consular Affairs, accessed on April 4, 2023, https://travel.state.gov/content/travel/en/ passports/how-apply.html.

2. "Student Visa," Australian Government Department of Home Affairs, accessed on April 4, 2023, https://immi.homeaffairs.gov.au/visas/getting -a-visa/visa-listing/student-500#Overview.

3. "Travel Advisories," US Department of State Bureau of Consular Affairs, accessed on April 14, 2023, https://travel.state.gov/content/travel/en/ traveladvisories/traveladvisories.html/.

4. "Smart Traveler Enrollment Program," US Department of State Bureau of Consular Affairs, accessed on May 5, 2023 https://step.state.gov/step/.
5. "Travelers' Health," Centers for Disease Control and Prevention, accessed on April 17, 2023, https://wwwnc.cdc.gov/travel.
6. "The International Lesbian, Gay, Bisexual, Trans, and Intersex Association," ILGA World, accessed on April 18, 2023, https://ilga.org
7. "Miranda Warning Equivalents Abroad," Law Library of Congress, Global Legal Research Center, accessed on May 5, 2023, https://sgp.fas.org/eprint/miranda.pdf.

CHAPTER 4

1. Kalvero Oberg, "Culture Shock: Adjustments to New Cultural Environments," *Practical Anthropology* 7, no. 4 (1960): 177–82, https://doi.org/10.1177/009182966000700405.
2. Stephen Bochner, "Culture Shock Due to Contact with Unfamiliar Cultures," *Online Readings in Psychology and Culture* 8, no. 1 (2003), https://doi.org/10.9707/2307-0919.1073.
3. Matt Hanson, "Wheatless Wanderlust," https://wheatlesswanderlust.com/, accessed July 14, 2023.

CHAPTER 6

1. Melanie L. D'Amico, "The Effects of Intensive Study Abroad and At Home Language Programs on Second Language Acquisition of Spanish," PhD dissertation, University of Florida, 2010, 31–37.
2. Lourdes Ortega, *Understanding Second Language Acquisition* (Hodder Education, 2009), 59–60.
3. Stephen D. Krashen, *Principles and Practice in Second Language Acquisition* (Pergamon Press, 1982), 20–22, http://www.sdkrashen.com/content/books/principles_and_practice.pdf.
4. Asunción Martínez-Arbelaiz, Elisabet Areizaga, and Carmen Camps, "An Update on the Study Abroad Experience: Language Choices and Social Media Abroad," *International Journal of Multilingualism* 14, no. 4 (2017): 350–65, https://doi.org/10.1080/14790718.2016.1197929.
5. Sally Sieloff Magnan and Michele Back, "Social Interaction and Linguistic Gain during Study Abroad," *Foreign Language Annals* 40, no. 1 (2007): 43–61.
6. Christina L. Isabelli-García, "Development of Oral Communication Skills Abroad" *Frontiers: the Interdisciplinary Journal of Study Abroad* 9, no. 1 (2003): 149–73, https://doi.org/10.36366/frontiers.v9i1.119.
7. Melanie L. D'Amico, "Exploring Changes in Second Language Willingness to Communicate during Short-Term Study Abroad," presentation, Kentucky Foreign Language Conference, Lexington, Kentucky, April 2016.

8. Joshua L. Pope, "Individual Differences in the Adoption of Dialectal Features during Study Abroad," in *Study Abroad and the Second Language Acquisition of Sociolinguistic Variation of Spanish*, ed. Sara Zahler, Bret Linford, and Avizia Y. Long (John Benjamins, 2023), 147–73.

9. Raquel Serrano, Elsa Tragant, and Àngels Llanes, "A Longitudinal Analysis of the Effects of One Year Abroad." *Canadian Modern Language Review* 68, no. 2 (2012): 138–63.

10. Rachel L. Shively and Andrew D. Cohen, "Development of Spanish Requests and Apologies during Study Abroad," *Íkala: Revista De Lenguaje y Cultura* 13, no. 20 (2008): 57–118.

11. Christina Isabelli-García, Jennifer Bown, John L. Plews, and Dan P. Dewey, "Language Learning and Study Abroad." *Language Teaching* 51, no. 4 (2018): 439–84.

12. "Cantonese" Must Go Travel, accessed December 12, 2022, https://www.mustgo.com/worldlanguages/cantonese/.

13. Barbara F. Freed, "What Makes Us Think That Students Who Study Abroad Become Fluent?" in *Second Language Acquisition in a Study Abroad Context*, ed. Barbara F. Freed (John Benjamins Publishing, 1995), 123–48; Ángles Llanes and Carmen Muñoz, "A Short Stay Abroad: Does It Make a Difference?" *System* 37, no. 3 (2009): 353–65, https://doi.org/10.1016/j.system.2009.03.001.

14. Kazuya Saito and Natsuko Shintani, "Do Native Speakers of North American and Singapore English Differentially Perceive Comprehensibility in Second Language Speech?" *TESOL Quarterly* 50, no. 2 (2015): 421–46.

15. Norman Segalowitz, Barbara Freed, Joe Collentine, Barbara Lafford, Nicole Lazar, and Manuel Díaz-Campos, "A Comparison of Spanish Second Language Acquisition in Two Different Learning Contexts: Study Abroad and the Domestic Classroom," *Frontiers: the Interdisciplinary Journal of Study Abroad* 10, no. 1 (2004): 1–18, https://doi.org/10.36366/frontiers.v10i1.130.

16. J. Cesar Felix-Brasdefer and Maria Hasler-Barker, "Complimenting in Spanish in a Short-Term Study Abroad Context," *System* (Linköping) 48 (2015): 75–85.

17. Hang Du, "Grammatical and Lexical Development during Study Abroad: Research on a Corpus of Spoken L2 Chinese," *Foreign Language Annals* 55, no. 4 (Winter 2022): 985–1005. Doi:https://doi.org/10.1111/flan.12631.

18. Stephanie M. Knouse, "The Acquisition of Dialectal Phonemes in a Study Abroad Context: The Case of the Castilian Theta," *Foreign Language Annals* 45, no. 4: 528–29.

19. Kimberly L. Geeslin and Aarnes Gudmestad, "The Acquisition of Variation in Second-Language Spanish: An Agenda for Integrating Studies of the L2 Sound System," *Journal of Applied Linguistics* 5, no. 2 (2008): 151.

CHAPTER 7

1. US Department of State, "The Fulbright Program," Fulbright, US Department of State, accessed on December 7, 2022, https://fulbrightspecialist .worldlearning.org/the-fulbright-program.

2. US Department of State, "Open Study/Research Award," Fulbright US Student Program, accessed on December 7, 2022, https://us.fulbrightonline .org/applicants/types-of-awards/study-research.

3. US Department of State, "English Teaching Assistant Programs," Fulbright US Student Program, accessed on December 7, 2022, https: //us.fulbrightonline.org/applicants/types-of-awards/english-teaching -assistant-awards.

4. JET Program, "Japan Exchange and Teaching Program," Embassy of Japan, accessed on December 7, 2022, https://jetprogramusa.org.

5. "What Are the Differences between High Context and Low Context Cultures?" Country Navigator, September 19, 2022, https://www.countrynavigator .com/blog/what-are-the-differences-between-high-context-and-low -context-cultures/#:~:text=The%20high%20and%20low%20context ,straightforward%20and%20explicit%20in%20communication.

6. "What Volunteers Do," Peace Corps, accessed on December 7, 2022, https:// www.peacecorps.gov/volunteer/what-volunteers-do.

7. "Is Peace Corps Right for Me," Peace Corps, accessed on December 7, 2022. https://www.peacecorps.gov/volunteer/is-peace-corps-right-for -me/.

CHAPTER 8

1. Celeste Kinginger, "Alice Doesn't Live Here Anymore: Foreign Language Learning and Identity Construction," in *Negotiation of Identities in Multilingual Contexts*, A. Pavlenko and A. Blackledge, eds. (Multilingual Matters LTD, 2004); Joshua Pope, "The Role of Social Networks in the Acquisition of a Dialectal Feature during Study Abroad," in *Issues in Hispanic and Lusophone Linguistic Series*, S. Sessarego and F. Tejedo-Herrero, eds. (John Benjamins, 2016), https://doi.org/10.1075/ihll.8.07pop.

2. Kevin McManus, "Relationships between Social Networks and Language Development during Study Abroad," *Language, Culture and Curriculum* 32, no. 3 (September 2019): 270–84, https://doi.org/10.1080/07908318 .2019.1661683.

3. Herbert H. Clark, "Conversation, Structure of," in *Encyclopedia of Cognitive Science*, L. Nadel, ed. (Wiley, 2006), https://doi.org/10.1002/0470018860 .s00228.

4. Simeon Floyd, "Conversation and Culture," *Annual Review of Anthropology* 50 (October 2021): 219–40, https://doi.org/10.1146/annurev-anthro-101819 -110158.

5. Alessandro Durante, "Universal and Culture-Specific Properties of Greetings," *Linguistic Anthropology* 7, no. 1 (June 2008): 63–97, https://doi.org /10.1525/jlin.1997.7.1.63.
6. Andrew D. Cohen, "Strategies for Learning and Performing L2 Speech Acts," *Intercultural Pragmatics* 2, no. 3 (September 2005): 275–301, https://doi .org/10.1515/iprg.2005.2.3.275.
7. "14 Apps That Will Actually Help You Make Friends," *Cosmopolitan*, September 21, 2022, https://www.cosmopolitan.com/sex-love/a24799641/ best-friendship-apps/.

CHAPTER 9

1. Bonny Norton, "Identity and Language Learning: Extending the Conversation" (Multilingual Matters, 2013), 4.
2. Xingsong Shi and Xiaoyan (Grace) Guo, "The Interplay between Identity Construction and L2 Investment during Study Abroad Programs: Cases of MBA Students from China," *Language and Intercultural Communication* 21, no. 2 (2021): 289–303, https://doi.org/10.1080/14708477.2020 .1837853.
3. Joshua Pope, "Individual Differences in the Adoption of Dialectal Features during Study Abroad," in *Study Abroad and the Second Language Acquisition of Sociolinguistic Variation in Spanish*, edited by Sara Zahler, Bret Linforn, and Avizia Long, 147–73 (John Benjamins, 2023), https://doi.org/10 .1075/ihll.37.05pop.

CHAPTER 10

1. "U.S. Study Abroad for Academic Credit Trends," Open Doors, accessed on February 6, 2023, https://opendoorsdata.org/data/us-study-abroad/u-s-study -abroad-for-academic-credit-trends/.
2. "Experiential Learning at FUA-AUF," Florence University of the Arts, accessed on February 13, 2023, https://fua.it/The-Schools/experiential-learning .html.
3. "Business Internship, Spanish Language and Latin American Studies," International Studies Abroad by WorldStrides, accessed on February 13, 2023, https://www.studiesabroad.com/destinations/latin-america/chile/valparaiso-and -vina-del-mar/business-internship-spanish-language--latin-american-studies.

BIBLIOGRAPHY

"14 Apps That Will Actually Help You Make Friends." *Cosmopolitan*, September 21, 2022, https://www.cosmopolitan.com/sex-love/a24799641/best -friendship-apps/.

Bochner, Stephen. "Culture Shock Due to Contact with Unfamiliar Cultures." *Online Readings in Psychology and Culture* 8, no. 1 (2003), https://doi.org /10.9707/2307-0919.1073.

"Business Internship, Spanish Language and Latin American Studies." *International Studies Abroad by WorldStrides*, accessed on February 13, 2023, https:// www.studiesabroad.com/destinations/latin-america/chile/valparaiso-and -vina-del-mar/business-internship-spanish-language--latin-american -studies.

"Cantonese." Must Go Travel, accessed December 12, 2022, https://www.mustgo .com/worldlanguages/cantonese/.

"CIEE." CIEE, accessed on September 8, 2023, ciee.org.

Clark, Herbert H., "Conversation, Structure of." In *Encyclopedia of Cognitive Science*, edited by L. Nadel. Wiley, 2006. https://doi.org/10.1002 /0470018860.s00228.

Cohen, Andrew D. "Strategies for Learning and Performing L2 Speech Acts." *Intercultural Pragmatics* 2, no. 3 (Sept. 2005): 275–301. https://doi .org/10.1515/iprg.2005.2.3.275.

D'Amico, Melanie L. "The Effects of Intensive Study Abroad and At Home Language Programs on Second Language Acquisition of Spanish." PhD diss., University of Florida, 2010.

———. "Exploring Changes in Second Language Willingness to Communicate during Short-Term Study Abroad." Presentation, Kentucky Foreign Language Conference, Lexington, Kentucky, April 2016.

Du, Hang. "Grammatical and Lexical Development during Study Abroad: Research on a Corpus of Spoken L2 Chinese." *Foreign Language Annals* 55, no. 4 (Winter 2022): 985–1005. doi:https://doi.org/10.1111/ flan.12631.

Durante, Alessandro. "Universal and Culture-Specific Properties of Greetings." *Linguistic Anthropology* 7, no. 1 (June 2008): 63–97. https://doi.org/10 .1525/jlin.1997.7.1.63.

"Educational Travel and Education Tours Abroad." WorldStrides, accessed on September 8, 2023, worldstrides.com.

"Experiential Learning at FUA-AUF." Florence University of the Arts, accessed on February 13, 2023, https://fua.it/The-Schools/experiential-learning .html.

Felix-Brasdefer, J. Cesar, and Maria Hasler-Barker. "Complimenting in Spanish in a Short-Term Study Abroad Context." *System* (Linköping) 48 (2015): 75–85.

"Flamenco: Artistic and Cultural Expression." ISA Seville Study Center, accessed August 28, 2023, https://www.studiesabroad.com/destinations /europe/spain/seville/spanish-language-culture--business/isvu1124/ flamenco-artistic-and-cultural-expression-562673.

Floyd, Simeon. "Conversation and Culture." *Annual Review of Anthropology* 50 (October 2021): 219–40. https://doi.org/10.1146/annurev-anthro-101819 -110158.

Freed, Barbara F. "What Makes Us Think That Students Who Study Abroad Become Fluent?" In *Second Language Acquisition in a Study Abroad Context*, edited by Barbara F. Freed. John Benjamins Publishing, 1995, 123–48.

Geeslin, Kimberly L., and Aarnes Gudmestad. "The Acquisition of Variation in Second-Language Spanish: An Agenda for Integrating Studies of the L2 Sound System." *Journal of Applied Linguistics* 5, no. 2 (2008): 151.

"Gilman Scholarship Program" Benjamin A. Gilman International Scholarship, accessed September 8, 2023, gilmanscholarship.org.

Hanson, Matt. "Wheatless Wanderlust," https://wheatlesswanderlust.com/, accessed July 14, 2023.

"How to Apply." US Department of State Bureau of Consular Affairs, accessed on April 4, 2023, https://travel.state.gov/content/travel/en/passports/how -apply.html.

"The International Lesbian, Gay, Bisexual, Trans, and Intersex Association." ILGA World, accessed on April 18, 2023, https://ilga.org.

"ISEP Study Abroad." ISEP, accessed on September 8, 2023, isepstudyabroad.org.

Isabelli-García, Christina L. "Development of Oral Communication Skills Abroad." *Frontiers: the Interdisciplinary Journal of Study Abroad* 9, no. 1 (2003): 149–73, https://doi.org/10.36366/frontiers.v9i1.119.

Isabelli-García, Christina, Jennifer Bown, John L. Plews, and Dan P. Dewey. "Language Learning and Study Abroad." *Language Teaching* 51, no. 4 (2018): 439–84.

JET Program. "Japan Exchange and Teaching Program." Embassy of Japan, accessed on December 7, 2022, https://jetprogramusa.org.

Kinginger, Celeste. "Alice Doesn't Live Here Anymore: Foreign Language Learning and Identity Construction." In *Negotiation of Identities in Multilingual Contexts*, edited by A. Pavlenko and A. Blackledge. Multilingual Matters LTD.

Knouse, Stephanie M. "The Acquisition of Dialectal Phonemes in a Study Abroad Context: The Case of the Castilian Theta." *Foreign Language Annals* 45, no. 4 (2012): 528–29.

Krashen, Stephen D. *Principles and Practice in Second Language Acquisition*. Pergamon Press, 1982, http://www.sdkrashen.com/content/books/principles _and_practice.pdf.

Llanes, Ángles, and Carmen Muñoz. "A Short Stay Abroad: Does It Make a Difference?" *System* 37, no. 3 (2009): 353–65, https://doi.org/10.1016/j .system.2009.03.001.

Magnan, Sally Sieloff, and Michele Back. "Social Interaction and Linguistic Gain during Study Abroad." *Foreign Language Annals* 40, no. 1 (2007): 43–61.

Martínez-Arbelaiz, Asunción, Elisabet Areizaga, and Carmen Camps. "An Update on the Study Abroad Experience: Language Choices and Social Media Abroad." *International Journal of Multilingualism* 14, no. 4 (2017): 350–65. https://doi.org/10.1080/14790718.2016.1197929.

McManus, Kevin. "Relationships between Social Networks and Language Development during Study Abroad." *Language, Culture and Curriculum* 32, no. 3 (Sept. 2019): 270–84. https://doi.org/10.1080/07908318.2019 .1661683.

"Miranda Warning Equivalents Abroad." The Law Library of Congress, Global Legal Research Center, accessed on May 5, 2023, https://sgp.fas.org/ eprint/miranda.pdf.

Norton, Bonny. "Identity and Language Learning: Extending the Conversation." Multilingual Matters, 2013.

Oberg, Kalvero. "Culture Shock: Adjustments to New Cultural Environments." *Practical Anthropology* 7, no. 4 (1960): 177–82. https://doi.org/10.1177 /009182966600700405.

Ortega, Lourdes. *Understanding Second Language Acquisition*. Hodder Education, 2009.

Peace Corps. "What Volunteers Do." Peace Corps, accessed on December 7, 2022, https://www.peacecorps.gov/volunteer/what-volunteers-do.

———. "Is Peace Corps Right for Me." Peace Corps, accessed on December 7, 2022. https://www.peacecorps.gov/volunteer/is-peace-corps-right-for -me/.

Pope, Joshua. "Individual Differences in the Adoption of Dialectal Features during Study Abroad." In *Study Abroad and the Second Language Acquisition of Sociolinguistic Variation in Spanish*, edited by Sara Zahler, Bret Linforn, and Avizia Long, 147–73. John Benjamins, 2023. https://doi.org/10.1075 /ihll.37.05pop.

———. "The Role of Social Networks in the Acquisition of a Dialectal Feature during Study Abroad." In *Issues in Hispanic and Lusophone Linguistic Series.* Edited by S. Sessarego and F. Tejedo-Herrero. John Benjamins Publishing, 2016. https://doi.org/10.1075/ihll.8.07pop

Saito, Kazuya, and Natsuko Shintani. "Do Native Speakers of North American and Singapore English Differentially Perceive Comprehensibility in Second Language Speech?" *TESOL Quarterly* 50, no. 2 (2015): 421–46.

Segalowitz, Norman, Barbara Freed, Joe Collentine, Barbara Lafford, Nicole Lazar, and Manuel Díaz-Campos. "A Comparison of Spanish Second Language Acquisition in Two Different Learning Contexts: Study Abroad and the Domestic Classroom." *Frontiers: The Interdisciplinary Journal of Study Abroad* 10, no. 1 (2004): 1–18, https://doi.org/10.36366/frontiers.v10i1.130.

Serrano, Raquel, Elsa Tragant, and Àngels Llanes. "A Longitudinal Analysis of the Effects of One Year Abroad." *Canadian Modern Language Review* 68, no. 2 (2012): 138–63.

Shi, Xingsong, and Xiaoyan (Grace) Guo. "The Interplay between Identity Construction and L2 Investment during Study Abroad Programs: Cases of MBA Students from China." *Language and Intercultural Communication* 21, no. 2 (2021): 289–303, https://doi.org/10.1080/14708477.2020.1837853

Shively, Rachel L., and Andrew D. Cohen. "Development of Spanish Requests and Apologies during Study Abroad." *Íkala: Revista De Lenguaje y Cultura* 13, no. 20 (2008): 57–118.

"Smart Traveler Enrollment Program." US Department of State Bureau of Consular Affairs, accessed on May 5, 2023 https://step.state.gov/step/.

"Student Visa." Australian Government Department of Home Affairs, accessed on April 4, 2023, https://immi.homeaffairs.gov.au/visas/getting-a-visa/visa-listing/student-500#Overview.

"Study and Volunteer in Ghana." ISEP Direct, University of Ghana, accessed September 5, 2023, https://search.isepstudyabroad.org/Program/Detail/fc1a6b13-07d7-4445-a487-2672676bd51c?ProgramTypeId=2.

"Summer Community Public Health." CIEE Santiago de los Caballeros, Dominican Republic, accessed September 5, 2023, https://www.ciee.org/go-abroad/college-study-abroad/programs/dominican-republic/santiago-de-los-caballeros/summer-community-public-health.

"Travel Advisories." US Department of State Bureau of Consular Affairs, accessed on April 14, 2023, https://travel.state.gov/content/travel/en/travcladvisories/traveladvisories.html/.

"Travelers' Health." Centers for Disease Control and Prevention, accessed on April 17, 2023, https://wwwnc.cdc.gov/travel.

US Department of State. "The Fulbright Program." Accessed on December 7, 2022, https://fulbrightspecialist.worldlearning.org/the-fulbright-program.

US Department of State. "English Teaching Assistant Programs." Fulbright US Student Program, accessed on December 7, 2022, https://us.fulbrightonline.org/applicants/types-of-awards/english-teaching-assistant-awards.

US Department of State. "Open Study/Research Award." Fulbright US Student Program, accessed on December 7, 2022, https://us.fulbrightonline.org/applicants/types-of-awards/study-research.

"US Study Abroad for Academic Credit Trends." Open Doors, accessed on February 6, 2023, https://opendoorsdata.org/data/us-study-abroad/u-s-study-abroad-for-academic-credit-trends/.

"What Are the Differences Between High Context and Low Context Cultures?" Country Navigator, September 19, 2022, https://www.countrynavigator.com/blog/what-are-the-differences-between-high-context-and-low-context-cultures/#:~:text=The%20high%20and%20low%20context,straightforward%20and%20explicit%20in%20communication.

INDEX

social norms, 28, 58–89, 68,
137, 154
sojourner, 119–121

teaching English, 101–102,
105–114, 116
technology: applications, 21,
24, 32, 45, 62, 72, 127,
131–133; computers/
laptops, 37, 43–44, 50, 81;
internet, 19–20, 38, 39, 42,
44, 54, 64, 79, 89, 91, 111,
133, 147; phones. *See* cell/
mobile phones
tourism, 11, 38–39, 48, 68, 71,
75–78, 82, 91, 119–121, 126
transcripts, 7, 33, 102, 155,
156. *See also* grades

US State
Department: embassies/
consulates, 19, 22, 24,
28–31; passports, 18, 19;
travel advisories, 4, 23

vaccines. *See*
healthcare: vaccines
visa, 17–22, 29–30, 104–105,
109–110
volunteering, 1, 9, 20, 115–117,
123, 150–154

working abroad, 1, 3, 11–13,
19–20, 27, 30, 39–40, 85,
91, 94, 101, 103–117, 120,
122–123, 150–154

About the Authors

Melanie L. D'Amico is an associate professor of Spanish and linguistics at Indiana State University. She holds a PhD in romance languages with a focus on Hispanic linguistics. Her research interests are in the area of second language acquisition focusing on study abroad, learning contexts, and language learning motivation. She has studied abroad at the University of Salamanca in Spain and the Torre di Babele language school in Rome, and she has led a program at the University of Salamanca.

Joshua Pope is an associate professor of Spanish at Doane University in Nebraska. He holds a PhD in applied Spanish linguistics. His research interests revolve around second language acquisition during study abroad, particularly when related to linguistic variation and identity. He studied abroad at the University of Alcalá de Henares in Spain and has co-led international experiences in Spain and Mexico.

www.ingramcontent.com/pod-product-compliance
Lightning Source LLC
Chambersburg PA
CBHW020354100426
42812CB00001B/61